The **Witches'** Almanac

SPRING 2005 — SPRING 2006

For the first time combining the mysterious wiccan and arcane secrets of an old England witch with one from New England

Prepared and edited by
ELIZABETH PEPPER and JOHN WILCOCK

CONTAINING pictorial and explicit delineations of the magical phases of the Moon together with full and complete information about astrological portents of the year to come and various aspects of occult knowledge enabling all who read to improve their lives in the old manner.

The Witches' Almanac, Ltd.

Publishers   Newport

Address all inquiries and information to

THE WITCHES' ALMANAC, LTD.

P.O. Box 1292

Newport, Rhode Island 02840-9998

ISBN: 1-881098-31-1

ISSN: 1522-3183

First Printing January 2005

Printed in the United States of America

Preface

Something in each of us responds in a profound way to one of the four elements. The old adage of "like seeks like" applies, and "to be in one's element" defines the most pleasurable state of being.

In the 5th century B. C., the Greek poet and philosopher Empedocles conceived the idea that all matter consists of only four forms: fire, earth, air, and water. They may change, combine or revert to their original nature, depending on two opposing forces. Empedocles wrote:

> *And these things never cease, but change forever.*
> *At one time all are joined and all is Love,*
> *And next they fly asunder, all is Strife.*

Magic is a decidedly personal matter. To recognize the element that belongs to you is essential in determining how to achieve a happy and successful life. Time passes swiftly and an awareness of where you belong in the grand scheme of nature smoothes the path to fulfillment. All four elements have attracted lore and legend, art and music as the tale of Western culture unfolds. Magical ways to divine the future, erase pain or make a wish come true find inspiration among them. Are you a creature of fire or of earth, air or water? Look deep into your secret heart to find the answer.

HOLIDAYS

Spring 2005 to Spring 2006

CONTENTS

ELIZABETH PEPPER & JOHN WILCOCK
Executive Editors

THEITIC
Managing Editor

BARBARA STACY & JEAN MARIE WALSH
Associate Editors

Astrologer	Dikki-Jo Mullen
Climatologist	Tom C. Lang
Technical Advisor	Robin Antoni
Digital Layout	Karen Marks
Research	Susan Chaunt
Sales	Ellen Lynch

All things are current found
On earthly ground,
Spirits, and elements
Have their descents.

Night and day, year on year,
High and low, far and near,
These are our own aspects,
These are our own regrets.

Ye gods of the shore,
Who abide evermore,
I see your far headland,
Stretching on either hand;

I hear the sweet evening sounds
From your undecaying grounds;
Cheat me no more with time,
Take me to your clime.

— HENRY DAVID THOREAU
*A Week on the Concord and
Merrimack Rivers* (1849)

today and tomorrow

By Oliver Johnson

GHOST TOWN WITH GHOSTS? Once a bustling place with 10,000 people, the old mining town of Bodie, California, was deserted by the 1950's when the gold ran out. The railroad had long vanished; most people just packed what they could into a truck and drove off. Families left behind what they couldn't carry, sparking a legend that anyone who removed any property could expect a string of bad luck. "The curse still exists today," says park ranger J. Brad Sturdivant. Some people take it so seriously that souvenirs are constantly returned. "We still get letters saying, "I'm sorry I took this; hoping my luck will change." The Skeptical Inquirer magazine is — well, skeptical. "Belief in curses is merely a superstition," writes Joe Nickell, "a form of magical thinking. Once it takes hold there is a tendency for any harmful occurrence to be counted as evidence for the belief, while beneficial events are ignored."

THE MAGIC MOUNTAIN. On a visibly higher level, something similar is happening in Australia. A growing awareness of the aborigines' sacred feelings for Ayers Rock has prompted tourists to return hundreds of stones taken from the lofty mountain. The acquisitive visitors claim to be fearful of the bad luck evoked by the souvenirs. The Ananga tribe, the Rock's official guardians, plan to use the returned pieces to build a memorial this year. The occasion marks the 20th anniversary of the Rock's restoration to the aborigines, as well as the return to its original name of Uluru. Packages arrive from all over the world.

Tribal insignia, Adelaide Museum, Australia

Some contain little more than soil or gravel; others hold rocks as big as 75 pounds. "Please return this to Uluru — six years' bad luck is enough," is a typical apology. Graeme Calmar,

6

chairperson of the local Ananga community, says, "A lot of people want a piece of the place because they know how great it is. But they haven't realized the true significance of the power of Uluru."

PRIMAL TIME. Explorations of ancient sites continue to redefine our notions of how far back civilization began. Recent excavations of magnificent Mayan royal ruins in Guatamala have stunned archaeologists, who had considered the era, c. 500 B.C., as one nurturing only simple farmers. Scientists believed that the Mayan culture flourished at such sites as Palenque and Tikal around 300 A.D. But the towering pyramids and sweeping plazas of Cival have yielded massive stone masks of a maize deity and a portrait of a Mayan king carved hundreds of years earlier. "We didn't even know there were kings then," says Francisco Estrada-Belli of Vanderbilt University.

And for the first time in Britain, archaeologists at a site in the Outer Hebrides have found what they claim are the oldest mummies in Europe — two embalmed bodies 3,500 years old believed to have been a king and queen. In another find of astonishing antiquity, archaeologists in South Africa report discovering the oldest known jewelry — 41 tiny beads of mollusk shells with holes bored for stringing and wearing. Discovered in the Blombos cave on the shores of the Indian Ocean, they are 75,000 years old.

TENDERNESS FOR TABBIES. Humankind's love of cats also joins the earlier - than - believed category. According to French archaeologists, such feelings may have been in effect as far back as 7500 B.C., the date of a grave recently excavated in Cyprus with a curled-up skeleton of a cat nestled with its master. "Early evidence of the taming of cats," suggests Dr. Jean-Denis Vigne of the Natural History Museum in Paris. He points out that this grave site preceded Egyptian feline worship by about 5,000 years. "In lieu of finding a bell around its neck," says the Smithsonian's Dr. Melinda A. Zeder, "this is about as solid evidence as one could have that cats held a special place in the lives and afterlives of people in this site."

GOLDEN RIVERS IN CENTRAL PARK. The works of artists Christo and Jeanne-Claude are truly magical. The husband and wife team is memorable for such massive ventures as "wrapping" the German Reichstag and the islands of Biscayne Bay. Now, after visionary projects in Australia, Japan, France and Switzerland, the Christo work will finally come to New York. In this year's Central Park effort, "The Gates," translucent saffron-colored cloth will line 23 miles of pathways. The panels will ripple softly when breezes prevail; viewed from above, the fluttering fabric will give the impression that the park shimmers with golden rivers. "Central Park is like the Mona Lisa of landscape architecture," says Christo, whose decade-long plan to fulfill this particular dream exemplifies what could be the credo of every true artist: *Never give up.*

PET THEORY. Rupert Sheldrake, a London doctor, researched his theory that pets — and especially cats — had telepathic means of knowing when a vet visit loomed. Almost all doctors reported canceled appointments because near the hour pets mysteriously vanished for awhile. "Some people say their dogs know when they are going to be taken for a walk, even at unusual times and even when they are in a different room, out of sight and hearing," Dr. Sheldrake reports. "If domestic animals are telepathic with their human owners, it seems likely that they are telepathic with each other in the wild."

YETI OR METI? The argument over whether the *yeti* — sometimes known as "the Abominable Snowman" — really exists has been revived by Yoshiteru Takahashi, the Japanese researcher. He says one of his team spotted such a figure in the mountains of Nepal, where they also discovered huge (35 x 30cm) footprints on Mt. Dhaulagiri at an elevation of 5,200 feet. Only a few weeks earlier, however, Makoto Nebuka of the Japanese Alpine Club announced that 12 years of fruitless searching had convinced him that the entire concept was a linguistic mistake. Nebuka explained that some dialects use *"yeti"* instead of the more common term *"meti"* to designate the Himalayan brown bear.

WATER COOLER CHI. Belief in *feng shui*, the controversial Chinese system of aligning the furniture in your house (and sometimes the house itself) has descended on the corporate world. A headline in the Los Angeles Times states that "More Big Firms are Quietly Using Feng Shui in their Work Spaces to Help Ensure Success." According to the story, consultants typically charge hundreds of dollars an hour to advise new locations for office equipment. The paper avers that *feng shui* is "equal parts science, philosophy and art. Its basis is the belief that everything in the universe has a life force of energy called *chi* that can be manipulated for beneficial results." Good *chi*, the article adds, "can generate new business and rising profits."

RAGS-TO-RICHES LANDSCAPE. From South Korea comes a report that the boyhood home of the president, Roh Moo Hyun, has become "an improbable tourist attraction." Rather than homage, the tourist ado seems more about geomancy — the supernatural way in which surroundings shape destiny. Up to 3,000 visitors a day come to Bongha, a tiny village near Pusan, many carrying compasses. The tourists calculate the angles of the sun and mountains to support their theory that the landscape played a specific part in the president's rags-to-riches success story. "There is something about this mountain that is different from others," says photographer Kim Hyong Su. And Kim Du Gyu, author of *Geomancy and Power*, says many more Koreans believe in geomancy than will admit it.

HEAR US, O ZEUS. In Greece, pagans have been facing off with the Orthodox Church. Greek pagans are petitioning for official recognition and the right to worship Zeus and other Hellenistic deities at traditionally sacred sites, including the Parthenon. According to the London Independent, Panayiotis Martinis, the pagans' spiritual leader, claims 100,000 adherents maintain the rites of Olympus. Many are contemptuous of the church. "Who were those early Christians?" scoffed one. "They were the great unwashed, they had no athletics, no culture, and only one book, the Bible."

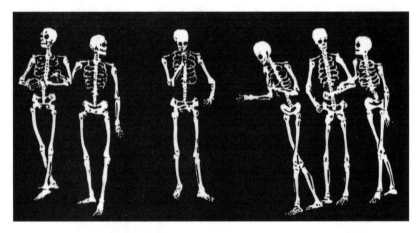

Between the idea
And the reality
Between the motion
And the act
Falls the Shadow.

— T. S. ELIOT

MOON GARDENING
BY PHASE

| Sow, transplant, bud and graft | | Plow, cultivate, weed and reap | |

NEW	First Quarter	FULL	Last Quarter	NEW
Plant above-ground crops with outside seeds, flowering annuals.	Plant above-ground crops with inside seeds.		Plant root crops, bulbs, biennials, perennials.	Do not plant.

BY PLACE IN THE ZODIAC

Fruitful Signs

Cancer — Most favorable planting time for all leafy crops bearing fruit above ground. Prune to encourage growth in Cancer.

Scorpio — Second only to Cancer, a Scorpion Moon promises good germination and swift growth. In Scorpio, prune for bud development.

Pisces — Planting in the last of the Watery Triad is especially effective for root growth.

Taurus — The best time to plant root crops is when the Moon is in the sign of the Bull.

Capricorn — The Earthy Goat Moon promotes the growth of rhizomes, bulbs, roots, tubers and stalks. Prune now to strengthen branches.

Libra — Airy Libra may be the least beneficial of the Fruitful Signs, but is excellent for planting flowers and vines.

Barren Signs

Leo — Foremost of the Barren Signs, the Lion Moon is the best time to effectively destroy weeds and pests. Cultivate and till the soil.

Gemini — Harvest in the Airy Twins; gather herbs and roots. Reap when the Moon is in a sign of Air or Fire to assure best storage.

Virgo — Plow, cultivate, and control weeds and pests when the moon is in Virgo.

Sagittarius — Plow and cultivate the soil or harvest under the Archer Moon. Prune now to discourage growth.

Aquarius — This dry sign of Air is perfect for ground cultivation, reaping crops, gathering roots and herbs. It is a good time to destroy weeds and pests.

Aries — Cultivate, weed, and prune to lessen growth. Gather herbs and roots for storage.

Consult our Moon Calendar pages for phase and place in the zodiac circle. The Moon remains in a sign for about two-and-a-half days. Match your gardening activity to the day that follows the Moon's entry into that zodiac sign.

EMPEDOCLES DEFINES

Empedocles was the first, so far as we know, to speak of the four elements:

> *Hear first the four roots of all things:*
> *Dazzling Zeus, life-bearing Hera, Aidoneus, and*
> *Nestis who moistens the springs of mortals with her tears.*

Peter Kingsley has shown in his recent book, *Ancient Philosophy, Mystery, and Magic: Empedocles and the Pythagorian Tradition*, that the names Aidoneus and Nestis both conceal and reveal two underworldly Deities, Hades and his bride Persephone, and that they are also Fire and Water. Zeus and his wife Hera, who are also Air and Earth, balance them in the overworld, rounding out the Circle of the Four Elements, symbolized by the serpent Ouroboros, who grasps his own tail with his mouth. In this circle, Divine husbands and wives stand opposite one another:

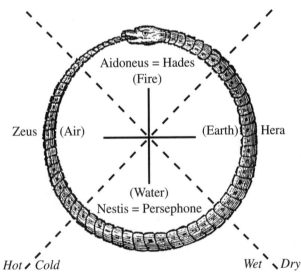

The four elements transmute one into another around the circle of this figure as their fundamental properties change: hot into cold and back again, or dry into wet and back again.

THE FOUR ELEMENTS

- Begin with Fire, which is both hot and dry. Moving downwards (or widdershins in the figure), transmute *overworldly* Fire — represented by the fire of the Sun — into Air by changing dry into wet. Though Fire is hot and *dry*, Air is hot and *wet*.
- Transmute again in the same direction by changing hot into cold, Air into Water. Though Air is *hot* and wet, Water is *cold* and wet.
- Transmute yet again by changing wet back into dry, Water into Earth. Though Water is cold and *wet*, Earth is cold and *dry*.
- Transmute one last time by changing cold back into hot, Earth into Fire. Though Earth is *cold* and dry, it is only Fire that is *hot* and dry.

Thus we have completed the Circle and returned to Fire, our point of departure. Yet it is now *underworldly* Fire, which is represented by the Fire of hot springs and volcanoes.

As we have moved widdershins around the circle, so we have moved downwards through the layers of Elements that make up the World. Fire rests on Air, Air rests on Water, Water rests on Earth, but Earth must also rest on something, and that something is once again Fire. As above, so below. It is Fire that rose up into the volcanic crater of Mount Etna 2,500 years ago and carried Empedocles out of the world of us mortals.

Of course, you can also move upwards, that is clockwise in the figure, by transmuting the elements in reverse order.

And what of the Center, where the union of Zeus and Hera intersects the union of Hades and Persephone? It is a point equidistant from all points on the circumference of the Circle that is our World. It is where a shaman goes to ascend and descend the World Tree. It is the point from which an astrologer calculates all angles. It is the inside of an alchemist's hermetically sealed vessel. It is a magician's best place of power.

A circle that you can draw with a compass on a piece of paper has only one center, for its radius and circumference are *finite*. But whenever the radius and circumference of a circle are *infinitely* distant (as they are in the Circle of our World), then *every* point within that circle is equally distant from its circumference — every point is its Center. When this is so, you do not need to traverse any space at all to stand at the Center of the World.

— ROBERT MATHIESEN

YEAR OF THE COCK
February 8, 2005 to January 29, 2006

Excitement generated by a Monkey Year persists as the Cock Year begins. The world is in a state of precarious balance now. Avoid taking unnecessary chances, for what is right today may be wrong tomorrow. The wisest course may be to play a waiting game. Expect complications while the Cock rules, for a simple matter is apt to take on epic proportions. Noble intentions and sincere dedication are lost in a welter of details. Yet a cheerful confidence prevails despite warnings of disaster. Patience and sound judgement will save the day.

Oriental astrological years run in cycles of twelve, each ruled by a symbolic animal. If you were born on or after the New Moon in Aquarius of the following years, you will display strength and confidence in the months ahead.

1909   1921   1933   1945   1957   1969   1981   1993   2005

The MOON Calendar

 is divided into zodiac signs rather than the more familiar Gregorian calendar.

2005   2006

 Bear in mind that new projects should be initiated when the Moon is waxing (from dark to full); when the Moon is on the wane (from full to dark), it is a time for storing energy and the wise person waits.

Please note that Moons are listed by day of entry into each sign. Quarters are marked, but as rising and setting times vary from one region to another, it is advisable to check your local newspaper, library or planetarium.

The Moon's Place is computed for Eastern Standard Time.

It was a lover and his lass

It was a lover and his lass,
With a hay, with a hoe and a hay nonie no,
That o're the green corn fields did pass,
In spring time, the only pretty ring time,
When birds do sing, hay ding a ding a ding;
Sweet lovers love the spring.

Between the acres of the rye,
With a hay, with a hoe and a hay nonie no,
These pretty country fools would lie,
In spring time, the only pretty ring time,
When birds do sing, hay ding a ding a ding,
Sweet lovers love the spring.

Then pretty lovers take the time,
With a hay, with a hoe and a hay nonie no,
For love is crowned with the prime,
In spring time, the only pretty ring time,
When birds do sing, hay ding a ding a ding,
Sweet lovers love the spring.

—THOMAS MORLEY (C.1557-1602)

aries | **March 21- April 20**

Mars *Cardinal Sign of Fire*

S	M	T	W	T	F	S
Mar. 20 2005 Vernal Equinox	21 *Cultivate and till the soil* Leo	22	23 *Make a careful choice* Virgo	24 *Summon a green wind*	25 seed moon Libra	26 WANING
27	28 *Plant and prune* Scorpio	29 *Follow your heart*	30 Sagittarius	31 *Nikolai Gogol born, 1809*	April 1 Capricorn	2 *Break a wicked spell*
3 *Set clocks ahead one hour* Aquarius	4	5 *Leave well enough alone*	6 *Cheer a lonely heart* Pisces	7 *Postpone decision*	8 Aries	9 WAXING
10 *Solve a mystery* Taurus	11 *Achieve a goal*	12 Gemini	13 *Seek a clear horizon*	14	15 *Emma Thompson born, 1959* Cancer	16
17 Leo	18 *Wear something red*	19 Virgo	20 *Shift an old pattern*			

Aesop's Fables   Ulm, 1476

The Vinegrower and His Sons

An old vinegrower was about to die, and he wanted his sons to
learn his trade. He called them to his bedside and said, "Boys, I'm
dying. Find all there is in my vineyard." They thought there was
treasure hidden there, and after their father died they took up picks
and shovels and dug up all the ground eagerly. They found no treasure, but now the ground was very well prepared for the vines,
which produced a huge number of grapes and made them rich.

MORAL: Hard work is a human's greatest treasure.

taurus	April 21- May 21

Venus — *Fixed Sign of Earth*

s	m	τ	w	τ	f	s
				April **21** *Hold a white stone* Libra	**22** *Celebrate goodness*	**23** *Watch the Moon rise*
24 (hare moon) Scorpio	**25** WANING	**26** Sagittarius	**27** *Prepare for the holiday*	**28** Capricorn	**29** *Michelle Pfeiffer born, 1958*	**30** *Feast on Roodmas Eve* Aquarius
May **1** BELTANE	**2** Pisces	**3** *Niccolo Machiavelli born, 1469*	**4** *Don't explain*	**5** *To judge is to harm* Aries	**6**	**7** *Connect with nature* Taurus
8 White Lotus Day	**9** WAXING Gemini	**10** *Honor departed souls*	**11**	**12** *Visit the spirit world* Cancer	**13** *Renew earth energy*	**14** *Spin the wheel* Leo
15 *Walk until weary*	**16**	**17** *Need not who needs not thee* Virgo	**18**	**19** *Work a healing spell* Libra	**20** *Pay homage to Venus*	**21** Scorpio

BAROQUE WIT AND WISDOM

The 17th century in France is called Le Grand Siècle, The Great Century, one of the high points in Western civilization. Duc Françoise de La Rochefoucauld (1613-1680) typified the brilliance of the era and lives on today, for his words appear in every book devoted to memorable quotations. Some of his thoughts:

Grace is to the body what clear thinking is to the mind.

Nothing is rarer than true goodness.

There is more self-love than love in jealousy.

To love but little is in love an infallible means of being beloved.

Absence diminishes moderate passions and increases great ones, as the wind blows out candles and fans fire.

Judged by most of its results, love is closer to hatred than to friendship.

Few people know how to be old.

It is less dangerous to injure most people than to treat them too kindly.

The greatest fault of a penetrating wit is to go beyond the mark.

The pleasure of love is in loving. We are happier in the passion we feel than in that we arouse.

We frequently forgive those who bore us, but cannot forgive those who we bore.

A man who finds no satisfaction in himself, seeks for it in vain elsewhere.

Confidence contributes more than wit to conversation.

♊ gemini · May 22- June 21

Mercury · *Mutable Sign of Air*

s	m	τ	w	τ	f	s
May **22** *Meet at moon rise*	**23** (dyad moon) Sagittarius	**24** WANING	**25**	**26** *Lenny Kravitz born, 1964* Capricorn	**27** *Fate may be unkind*	**28** *Learn how to forget* Aquarius
29 Oak Apple Day	**30** Pisces	**31** *Observe the Old Ways*	June **1** Aries	**2** *Onward and upward*	**3** Taurus	**4** *Do not cross running water*
5 *Night of the Watchers* Gemini	**6**	**7** WAXING	**8** *Joan Rivers born, 1933* Cancer	**9** *Say the secret word*	**10** *Drift for a while* Leo	**11** *Try before you trust*
12 Virgo	**13** *Discover a mare's nest*	**14**	**15** *Consult a seer* Libra	**16**	**17** *Measure the odds* Scorpio	**18** *Sing before breakfast*
19 *Gather wild herbs*	**20** *Celebrate Midsummer Eve* Sagittarius	**21** SUMMER SOLSTICE ✳				

Midsummer Fire

bonfire, n. (ME. bonefire, banefire, orig. a fire of bones.)
Webster's Dictionary, 1934

Ceremonial bonfires celebrated holidays throughout Europe and the British Isles. The events began in pagan times and have persisted to the present. Folklorist Jacob Grimm believed them to be the survival of a once dominant religion which sought to waken latent psychic power and perception by means of ritual.

Summer solstice, the moment when the sun reaches its zenith and appears to stand still, was always an occasion for building great fires. Midsummer Night, or St. John's Eve as it came to be known under Christian domination, was observed in Britain with strict rules. A chronicle of 1515 records that "in the worship of St. John, the people make three manners of fires: one of clean bones and no wood, and that is called a bone fire; another of clean wood and no bones, and that is called a wood fire; and the third is made of wood and bones, and is called St. John's fire."

A Cornish version of Midsummer Fire occurs annually on June 23rd. When darkness falls, a beacon fire is kindled at St. Ives. Then all through the night a chain of bonfires blazes forth, one after another, across the length of the land. As each fire is lit, a master of ceremonies recites a blessing in the old Cornish language that roughly translates to:

Now set the pyre at once on fire,
Let flames aspire in his high name!

A woman chosen to be Lady of the Flowers tosses a bouquet of herbs, wildflowers and leafy boughs on the fire with the invocation:

In a bunch together bound
Flowers for burning here are found,
Both good and ill;
Thousandfold let good seed spring,
Wicked weeds fast withering.

The floral tribute contains vervain, rue, lavender, meadowsweet, St. John's wort, yellow and white daisies, orpine, feverfew, red clover mixed with branches of oak, ash and rowan.

Villagers merrily dance, young couples in love join hands and leap over the flames for good luck. The ashes of each fire are collected in a sack to form the base for the beacon fire the following year.

cancer | June 22- July 23

Moon | *Cardinal Sign of Water*

s	m	т	w	т	f	s
		Draw down the Moon 👉	June **22** (mead moon) Capricorn	**23** WANING	**24** *St. John's Day* Aquarius	**25** *Trust your intuition*
26 *Peter Lorre born, 1904* Pisces	**27**	**28** ◐ Aries	**29**	**30** *Lena Horn born, 1917* Taurus	July **1** *Wear an amulet*	**2** *Face the music* Gemini
3 *Harm hatch, harm catch*	**4** *The old fox smiles*	**5** Cancer	**6** ●	**7** WAXING	**8** *Time to seek an answer* Leo	**9** *Follow your bliss*
10 *Find the still point* Virgo	**11**	**12** *Reap a wild harvest*	**13** *Yours is the magic* Libra	**14** ◑	**15** Scorpio	**16** *Keep all channels clear*
17 Sagittarius	**18** *Follow the current*	**19** *Whistle up the wind* Capricorn	**20**	**21** (wort moon) Aquarius	**22** *Enjoy a magic moment*	**23** Pisces

23

VESTAL VIRGINS

At the foot of Palatine Hill, deep in the Roman Forum, six little girls played with fire. The play was serious business, though, for these handpicked maidens, six to ten years old, were learning the duties, rituals and mysteries connected with their apprenticeship as Vestal Virgins in ancient Rome. Ten years of learning, ten years of serving, ten years of teaching; such was the scheduled life for each team of recruits to the service of Vesta, Roman Goddess of the Hearth. The rewards were inviting — life in a sumptuous mansion with slaves-in-waiting, places of honor at theaters and other public spectacles, the respect and adoration of the people. And the duties were not so onerous. Fetching water from a sacred spring for ceremonial sprinklings, sweeping the shrine, guarding sacred objects, preparing and offering sacrifices, saying daily prayers for the well-being of the Empire. And, of course, keeping the mystic flame continuously alight and protected in times of danger, for it was believed that extinguishing the fire would bring disaster to the Roman Empire.

♌ leo | July 24- August 23

Sun   *Fixed Sign of Fire*

s	m	т	w	т	ƒ	s
July **24** *Cast a cold eye*	**25** *Gypsies gather tonight* Aries	**26** *Sandra Bullock born, 1964*	**27** ◐	**28** *Habits are chains* Taurus	**29**	**30** *Fly by night* Gemini
31 Lughnassad Eve	Aug. **1** LAMMAS ✳ Cancer	**2** *Fulfill all duties*	**3** *Free your soul*	**4** ● Leo	**5** WAXING	**6** *Robert Mitchum born, 1917* Virgo
7 *Practice sorcery now*	**8** *Observe the tides*	**9** Libra	**10** *Deep calls to deep*	**11** *Dare to be yourself*	**12** ◑ Scorpio	**13** DIANA'S DAY
14 Sagittarius	**15** *Stretch a point*	**16** Capricorn	**17** *Hail to the red wind*	**18** *Consult the Tarot* Aquarius	**19** ◯ barley moon	**20** WANING Pisces
21 *Look before you leap*	**22**	**23** *Keep a low profile*				

25

THOTH TIME

The West's first magus is undoubtedly Thoth, ancient Egypt's god of wisdom and magic. His symbolic ibis-headed figure appears on the earliest monuments of the Old Kingdom, and it is speculated that the concept of Thoth as a divinity was established before 4000 B.C.

From that remote date to the turn of the Common Era, Thoth retained his essential character as patron of learning and keeper of arcane lore. First century magical texts, including the celebrated Emerald Tablet, were often attributed to Hermes Trismegistus, a designation honoring Thoth as three times greater than his Greek divine equivalent. Greeks and Romans were in awe of the spiritual achievements and occult disciplines preserved by the far-older Egyptian culture. The 18th-century philologist Court de Gebelin believed the Tarot cards comprised a sacred and secret doctrine known to the Egyptians. He called the deck "The Book of Thoth."

Thoth is the Greek name for Egypt's divine Scribe. He is identified in hieroglyphics as Tehuti, a Moon god — He who dispels darkness with his light. The baboon, a highly intelligent and social animal, was his creature. Thoth represented knowledge, good order, invention, and something more — the sense of magic. A hint of this theme is recorded in the Pyramid Texts: *Thoth who gives to thee thy heart (understanding); that thou mayest remember what thou hadst forgotten.*

A thousand years later in the reign of Ramses II, a poet addressed Thoth:

O thou sweet Well for the thirsty in the desert! It is closed up for him who speaks, but it is open for him who keeps silence. When he who keeps silence comes, lo he finds the Well.

Perhaps it was in the spirit of Thoth, also known as the measurer of time, that the Egyptians devised the earliest known calendar. The arbitrary scheme of twelve months and 365 days, with variations, has been in continual use ever since. When the Dog Star rises in the east before dawn and the Nile overflows its banks, the Egyptian New Year is born. The first month is named for Thoth, a traditional time for divination and magical work. Translated to our current calendar system, the first day of Thoth begins at dawn on August 29. Certain days of this month are more appropriate for ritual than others. A papyrus in the British Museum's vast collection (this one is No. 10,474) lists the favorable days of Thoth as August 29 and 30, September 2, 6, 7, 14, 15, 16, 21, 22, 24, 25, 26, 27.

virgo — August 24–September 23

Mercury   *Mutable Sign of Earth*

s	**m**	**т**	**w**	**т**	**ƒ**	**s**
			Aug. **24** *Choose the right key* Taurus	**25**	**26** ◐ Gemini	**27** *Study the Old Ways*
28 *Delay decision* Cancer	**29** *Day of Thoth*	**30** *Cameron Diaz born, 1972*	**31** Leo	Sept. **1** *Three is the charm*	**2**	**3** ● Virgo
4 WAXING	**5** *Time is like fire* Libra	**6** *Pay your debts*	**7** *Criss-cross, thy loss*	**8** Scorpio	**9** *To the pure, all is pure*	**10** Sagittarius
11 ◑	**12** *H.L. Mencken born, 1880* Capricorn	**13**	**14** *Work within limits* Aquarius	**15** *Clarify a sad mistake*	**16** Pisces	**17** wine moon
18 WANING Aries	**19** *Leave all to fate*	**20**	**21** *Bless all creatures* Taurus	**22** AUTUMNAL EQUINOX	**23** *Guard your secrets* Gemini	

with the tree's roots for nutrients in the soil. Ivy growing up the walls of buildings promotes dryness within and serves as a protective shield against the atmosphere. Its botanical name in Latin is *Hedera helix* and describes ivy's spiral form of growth, for *helix* means "to turn round."

The rich deep evergreen color and climbing spiral action inspired the ancients to identify ivy with immortality, resurrection and rebirth. The classical gods of wine, the Greek Dionysos and his Roman counterpart Bacchus, are often depicted wearing crowns of ivy. This association with the grapevine, which also grows in spiral form, gave ivy the reputation for diminishing drunkenness, for it was thought that one spiral reversed the power of the other. Ivy came to symbolize fidelity and one perfect leaf collected when the moon was one day old was a useful amulet in matters of love.

the
ivy

Oh roses for the flush of youth, and laurel for the perfect prime; but pluck an ivy branch for me grown old before my time.
— CHRISTINA ROSSETTI

IVY, *gort*, represents the eleventh consonant of the Celtic Tree alphabet and rules from September 30 to October 27. European folklore has credited ivy with mythic qualities since classical times.

When ivy trails along the ground it remains weak and does not produce fruit, but when it climbs using a tree or a wall for support, it grows increasingly stronger putting out flowers in autumn and berries in the spring. Birds feast on ivy's purple-black berries scattering the seeds to form new plants in the soft spring earth. Ivy draws no nourishment from the tree it climbs nor do its underground roots seriously compete

IVY. *Hedera helix*

libra
September 24- October 23

Venus   *Cardinal Sign of Air*

s	m	T	w	T	F	s
						Sept. 24 *Strike a balance*
25 Cancer	**26** *Make up your mind*	**27**	**28** *Learn by heart* Leo	**29** *Don a thinking cap*	**30** *Reduce expenses* Virgo	**Oct. 1**
2 *Prime the pump*	**3** Libra	**4** WAXING	**5** *Time is flying* Scorpio	**6** *Avoid flatties*	**7** Sagittarius	**8** *Sigourney Weaver born, 1949*
9 *Consult an elder*	**10** Capricorn	**11** *Carry a talisman*	**12** Aquarius	**13** *Lend a helping hand*	**14** *Wear an amulet* Pisces	**15** *Beware hidden danger*
16 *Eugene O'Neill born, 1888* Aries	**17** blood moon	**18** WANING Taurus	**19** *Make a circle of leaves*	**20** Gemini	**21** *Anticipate change*	**22** *A brown wind sighs* Cancer

G. P. Jacomb Hood, 1889

FIREGAZING

The divining art of pyromancy or firegazing has been practiced for centuries. Reading the message of fire was often the duty of a religious priesthood or of professional augurs, but as the method was simple many individuals performed the rite themselves. Anyone wanting a fiery omen to foretell the outcome of a proposed venture could proceed in the following manner:

When the hearth fire is reduced to glowing embers, cast upon it a handful of pounded dried peas. If the peas catch fire quickly and burn silently, the omen is good. Should the flames leap high and burn brightly, forming an upright triangle, success is assured. Failure to burn, heavy smoke, crackling, and erratic flames bending from side to side are all evil omens. And if the fire blazes swiftly and suddenly goes out,

it is a warning that danger surrounds your question.

Another kind of firegazing offers a deeper and less obvious source of revelation. This exercise of presage took the form of a game in colonial America. When a family gathered before the fireplace of an evening and one person seemed withdrawn and silent, the cheerful question, "What do you see in the fire, m'dear, what do you see in the fire?" would be asked. The answer had to be three fire images, quickly found and announced without second thoughts: for instance, "a ship at sea, a marigold, a knight who threatens me." All the family would comment, offer interpretations or guess what the visions foretold. As each family member in turn was challenged to seek pictures in the fire, the atmosphere took on a warm glow, and laughter and good spirits often restored the troubled one.

But the game of firegazing wasn't restricted to family activity. The old custom could serve the local witch as well.

If a nervous visitor found it awkward to confide a problem and the witch failed to divine it by psychic means, the familiar question would serve to lessen tension. The forthcoming answer chosen from the haphazard patterns of a hearth fire provided a source of conversation and revealed hints of the difficulty. Soon the whole story would tumble out.

But even if you never use a fire as an oracle, finding images and omens in flames or in glowing embers is a strangely rewarding pastime. The stimulation of imagination is its own reward.

scorpio October 24-November 22

Pluto | *Fixed Sign of Water*

s	m	т	w	т	f	s
	Oct. 24	25 *Toss a token in the sea* Leo	26	27 *Bear no malice* Virgo	28 *Trust your instincts*	29 *Protect your soul*
30 *Return to Standard Time 2am* Libra	31 Eve of HALLOW-MAS	Nov. 1 Samhain Scorpio	2 WAXING	3 *Fly by night*	4 Sagittarius	5 *Fate takes charge*
6 *Beckon an astral spirit* Capricorn	7	8 Aquarius	9 *Work a candle spell*	10 *Richard Burton born, 1925* Pisces	11 *Value a good friend*	12 *Make an effort* Aries
13 *Avoid extremes*	14 *Go back in time* Taurus	15 snow moon	16 WANING ✶ HECATE NIGHT	17 Gemini	18 *Music eases stress*	19 *Make haste slowly* Cancer
20 *Well begun is half done*	21 Leo	22 *Geraldine Page born, 1924*				

FRUIT AND FIRE

Ancient Romans loved pomp and ceremony. That unique sense of occasion extended to the home where Vesta, goddess of fire, presided over hospitality. Her light spirit added entertainment to an evening's repast. There's drama in presenting flaming fare. Guests enjoy the flickering sight, and with fruit desserts in the offing the sweet aroma adds further charm. Herewith three classic recipes that are delectable, amazingly easy to prepare. Be sure to whisper Vesta's name as you set the warm spirit ablaze.

Bananas Flambé

4 tablespoons butter
1 teaspoon grated lemon rind
1 tablespoon lemon juice
4 ripe bananas
4 tablespoons dark brown sugar
1/4 cup warm rum

Preheat the oven to 350 degrees. Put the butter, lemon rind and juice in a baking dish and place it in the oven for about 2 minutes or until the butter is melted. Remove and stir. Add the whole peeled bananas to the dish, turning to coat them with the butter mixture. Sprinkle with brown sugar and bake for about 15 minutes. Bring the baking dish to the table immediately, pour over the warm rum, ignite and spoon the burning rum over the bananas. Serves 4.

Cherries Jubilee

1 can pitted black cherries
1 tablespoon sugar
1 tablespoon cornstarch
1/4 cup warmed kirsch or other fruit
    liqueur
Vanilla ice cream

Drain cherries, reserving the juice. Mix sugar and cornstarch and add 1 cup of the juice a little at a time. Cook 3 minutes, stirring constantly. Add the cherries, stir, and heat for 1 minute longer. Bring the pan to the table at once and add the warm kirsch to the pan. Ignite the liqueur and spoon it over the cherries and serve over the ice cream. Serves 6.

Peaches Flambé

1 cup sugar
1 and 1/2 cups water
6 peeled peaches
1/4 cup warmed Cointreau or other
    fruit liqueur

Dissolve sugar in water and simmer for 10 minutes, stirring from time to time. Add peaches and simmer for 5 minutes or until tender. Add warmed liqueur, ignite, and spoon over the peaches. Serves 6.

sagittarius November 23-December 21

Jupiter   *Mutable Sign of Fire*

s	m	t	w	t	f	s
			Nov. **23**	**24** *Yield to higher forces* Virgo	**25**	**26** *Delay decision* Libra
27 *Pay homage to the oak tree*	**28** *Jon Stewart born, 1962*	**29** Scorpio	**30** *Consult the Tarot*	Dec. **1** Sagittarius	**2** WAXING	**3** *Blaze a trail* Capricorn
4	**5** *Heed a white wind* Aquarius	**6** *Keep wits about you*	**7** *Laughter heals* Pisces	**8**	**9** Aries	**10** *Take a respite now*
11 *Choose another path*	**12** Taurus	**13** *Ignore the vulgar*	**14** *There was but one of you* Gemini	**15** oak moon	**16** WANING Cancer	**17** Saturnalia begins
18 *Betty Grable born, 1916*	**19** Leo	**20** Eve of Yule	**21** WINTER SOLSTICE Virgo			

33

ELEMENTAL OF FIRE

THE ZOOLOGICAL salamander is an unremarkable little amphibian that resembles a lizard. But its mythological counterpart has a uniquely wondrous quality — a body so icy that it can withstand flames.

Belief concerning the salamander's marvelous virtue existed in ancient Egypt and Babylon. In Greece, Aristotle wrote that the salamander "not only walks through fire, but puts it out in doing so." Roman naturalist Pliny described the creature as "so intensely cold as to extinguish fire by its contact, in the same way that ice does." A medieval monk kept the myth alive by recording: "This animal is the only one which puts the flames out. Indeed, it lives in the middle of the blaze without being hurt and without

Seal of King Francis I

being burnt." The scholarly monarch Francis I of France chose as his emblem a salamander in flames with the motto: "I nourish and extinguish."

But the mythical lizard gained enduring magical significance in the Renaissance, when Paracelsus, the great Swiss magus, declared the salamander to be the Elemental of Fire. The doctrine of Paracelsus held that Elementals were primal beings inhabiting the classical four roots of matter: gnomes of Earth, sylphs of Air, and undines of Water. The salamander of Fire symbolically expressed a spark igniting action, purification, and transformation. Paracelsus equated the essence of fire with the power of imagination in the human spirit: "that explosive flare that lights up the inner spaces, revealing meaning."

No great leap of imagination is required to guess the origin of the fabulous salamander, given the zoological creature's actual habits. The tiny lizard likes to cozy up in a log with a nice damp hole. And if such a log turns up in a fireplace and the salamander is rudely awakened by flames, its movements are less frolic than frantic, a usually successful scramble for life.

♑ capricorn December 22- January 20

Saturn   *Cardinal Sign of Earth*

s	m	т	w	т	f	s
				Dec. **22** *Time for a break*	**23**	**24** *The cold endures* Libra
25 *Haze circles the Moon*	**26** Scorpio	**27** *Watch your diet*	**28** *Feed the wild birds* Sagittarius	**29** *Invent another world*	**30** Capricorn	**31** WAXING
Jan. **1** 2006	**2** *Improve your vision* Aquarius	**3** *Relax at proper time*	**4** Pisces	**5** *Enjoy life*	**6** Aries	**7** *Lend a hand*
8 *Weave a spell* Taurus	**9** Day of Janus	**10** Gemini	**11** *Alexander Hamilton born, 1755*	**12** *Cut the knot*	**13** *Maintain reserve* Cancer	**14** wolf moon
15 WANING Leo	**16** *Blessings overflow*	**17** *Seek a fortune*	**18** Virgo	**19** *Dolly Parton born, 1946*	**20** *Pain has limits* Libra	

TAROT'S JUDGEMENT

Ancien Tarot de Marseilles 1761

Most sources identify the winged figure as the archangel Gabriel, bursting forth from the clouds with banner and trumpet in hand. The Old and New Testament mark Gabriel as the spirit of truth, angel of death, and prince of fire and thunder. The Koran calls him "the angel of revelations, who writes down the divine decrees." Gnostic and Hermetic strains of Christian thought are evident in the Marseilles deck.

Three humans, two living and one dead, respond to the trumpet's blast. The message of the card is to awaken, rise above terrestrial limits, transcend the world of matter.

When the No. 20 key turns up in a reading, it often represents an end and a beginning, spiritual atonement and renewal. Thought has many levels and we can achieve truth if we are aware enough to perceive it.

aquarius January 21-February 19

Uranus   *Fixed Sign of Air*

s	m	т	w	т	ʄ	s
						Jan. **21** *Conceit dooms now*
22	**23** *Divine by cup* Scorpio	**24** *Recall absent friends*	**25** Sagittarius	**26** *Not worth a curse*	**27** *Fair is foul* Capricorn	**28** *Settle a claim*
29 Year of the Dog Aquarius	**30** WAXING	**31** Pisces	Feb. **1** *Eve of Oimelc*	**2** ❋ CANDLE- MAS Aries	**3** *Collect blessed water*	**4** *Clear the decks* Taurus
5	**6** *Aaron Burr born, 1756* Gemini	**7** *Make good order*	**8** *Sweep away debris*	**9** *Amy Lowell born, 1874* Cancer	**10**	**11** *Tears before bedtime* Leo
12 *Clouds gather*	**13** storm moon	**14** WANING Virgo	**15**	**16** *Purify all* Libra	**17** *Blow away cobwebs*	**18** *Pay close attention*
19 Scorpio						

FIRE SPIRITS

Everyone is intrigued by the dancing display of fire, but few attune to its deeper mystical uses. We all love the flickering of flames, the hum of burning wood, and the mutability of heat — at one remove evoking comfort, closer evoking fear. But the wise acquire ancient techniques of observing fire in a mindful, rewarding way.

When you look at the flame, become aware of its parts — the tips dancing among the deeper merged base of the fire. Sometimes they move with air currents, sometimes in harmony with background sounds. The informed witch can become one with fire and knows that messages derive from its movement, color and shadows.

The elementals of fire contribute to our passion for life, offering the gifts of drive, assertiveness, and will. When we feel weakness in such areas, it is wise to reaffirm our relationship with these elementals, the Salamanders. This bonding is most effective in noon sunlight or at midnight before the fireplace.

Begin the ritual with a red candle anointed with oil; wax is food for the Salamanders. When you light the wick say aloud:

Fire of change I now light
Grant to me the gift of sight.

Gaze into the candle flame and allow it to glow in your mind's eye. The brightness will grow until it encompasses all your inner vision. Feel safely embraced by the warmth of the light. Allow yourself to know the element and its secrets. Encourage your mind to accept all manner of pictures and sounds. See the shadows and flickering flames become images, hear the faint sound of burning become the voices of the Salamanders.

Remember that the elementals converse with us in ways alien to most humans. An aware person will practice this art of firegazing over time and learn to uncover the secrets and strengths guarded by these mighty elementals.

— THEITIC

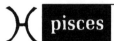 **pisces** February 20 -March 20

Neptune　　　　*Mutable Sign of Water*

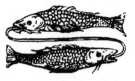

s	m	т	w	т	ƒ	s
	Feb. **20** *Plan a pleasure garden*	**21** Sagittarius	**22** *Chopin born, 1810*	**23** Capricorn	**24** *Celebrate the senses*	**25** *Obey a whim* Aquarius
26 *Beg the question*	**27** Pisces	**28** WAXING	Mar. **1**	**2** *Fortuna Major* Aries	**3** *Trust common sense*	**4** *Mind over matter* Taurus
5 *Take no risks*	**6** Gemini	**7** *Scry for an answer*	**8** *Meet a new challenge* Cancer	**9**	**10** *Charm a stranger*	**11** *Remain flexible* Leo
12 *Spend time alone*	**13** Virgo	**14** chaste moon	**15** WANING	**16** *Expect a backlash* Libra	**17** *Mia Hamm born, 1972*	**18** *Wild birds return* Scorpio
19 *Renew energy*	**20** *Head for the woods* Sagittarius					

Moon Cycles

A New Moon rises with the Sun,
Her waxing half at midday shows,
The Full Moon climbs at sunset hour,
And waning half the midnight knows.

NEW	2006	FULL	NEW	2007	FULL
January 29		January 14	January 19		January 3
February 27		February 13	February 17		February 2
March 29		March 14	March 18		March 3
April 27		April 13	April 17		April 2
May 27		May 13	May 16		May 2/31
June 25		June 11	June 14		June 30
July 25		July 10	July 14		July 29
August 23		August 9	August 12		August 28
September 22		September 7	September 11		September 26
October 22		October 6	October 11		October 26
November 20		November 5	November 9		November 24
December 20		December 4	December 9		December 23

Life takes on added dimension when you match your activities
to the waxing and waning of the Moon. Observe the sequence
of her phases to learn the wisdom of constant change within
complete certainty.

Window on the Weather

The summer and winter of 1987 brought dry weather to the northern Rockies, the product of a two-year El Niño event. Fires resulted, raging through more than 100,000 acres in and around Yellowstone National Park. A special committee of scientists and policymakers convened and concluded that though weather conditions continued dry, so much had already burned that the remaining undergrowth would not be much of a threat the following summer. But when El Niño moved on, it was replaced by a strong La Niña, a rare occurrence and one that favored even drier conditions across the northern Rockies. Contrary to predictions, during the summer of 1988 fires of unprecedented magnitude swept through the Yellowstone ecosystem of Idaho, Montana and Wyoming. Throughout the summer, relative humidity levels frequently dropped to 10 percent in both the air and in the remaining combustible undergrowth. The result, a conflagration that scorched 1.4 million acres and prompted chastened scientists to re-evaluate the conditions that make wildfires likely. Now they conclude that the strongest factor defining susceptibility to fire is the overall global weather pattern. This year, the lingering effects of a weak El Niño result in a somewhat higher fire likelihood in the northern Rockies, Washington and Oregon.

— TOM C. LANG

SPRING

MARCH 2005. An El Niño episode will bring a wetter than normal spring to the East this year. Atlantic breezes, associated with offshore storms, will be mild. Snow will change to rain near the coast. Inland locations will receive above-normal snowfall from central Pennsylvania to interior Maine. One particularly strong storm will bring high winds to much of the East by the 15th. In the deep South, the tornado season will be perilous this year. Arkansas, Alabama, Tennessee and Georgia will be especially vulnerable. Historically, Alabama has the highest incidence of intense, long-lasting tornadoes. Southern California will be wetter than normal, with the San Francisco Bay area lashed by 50 mile-per-hour winds around the 10th. The northern Plains and Great Lake States will be relatively cold and dry.

APRIL 2005. April is a cool month, with full spring weather yet to arrive. Plenty of energy exists for storm formation. Thunderstorms can turn violent, with tornadoes spawned throughout the South and in the southern Plains.

A widespread twister outbreak makes national headlines, and great care should be taken around the 20th. Cold air lingers in northern and western Valleys. Planting is delayed in these areas until month's end. Between the 15th and 22nd, a late-season snowstorm blankets California's Sierra Nevada, the Colorado Rockies, and northern New England's mountains. Warm, humid conditions prevail in Florida, while desert flowers spring to life in the Great Basin of the West. Southern California is drenched by rain around the 30th.

MAY 2005. The peak of tornado season; several large outbreaks can be anticipated this month. People in the Central Plains and Ohio Valley should be alert for changing late-afternoon weather conditions. Approaching cold fronts should be keenly observed for signs of thunderstorm development — isolated tornadoes are sometimes spawned at that time and can form quickly between 4 p.m. and 8 p.m. Elsewhere, the weather is quiet. The Northeast spends the month covered in clouds, fog and drizzle with one long rainstorm midmonth. The West Coast experiences brisk Pacific breezes. Several large brush fires may break out in Florida.

SUMMER

JUNE 2005. Storm activity shifts to the northern tier of states, with thunderstorms roaming from the Dakotas to New England. Several times high winds and hail sweep the landscape but little damage is reported. Coastal cities experience placid weather. East winds keep temperatures cool and widespread mist and fog belie the calendar, though summer is merely weeks away. From the Carolinas south, an early-season heat wave brings temperatures to the 90s before slightly cooler air arrives around the 20th. Pleasantly warm days and cool nights are enjoyed in California, and the Central Valley receives a fine stretch of spring weather. Abundant crop yields are expected after plentiful winter rainfall.

JULY 2005. Midsummer heat prevails throughout the Southeast, Great Plains and interior West Coast. Thunderstorms erupt in the afternoon a few miles inland on both coasts of Florida. Rainfall is substantial with these storms. Atlanta receives above-normal rainfall with thunderstorms forming at about sunset. Summer weather finally arrives in the Northeast. Frequent cool fronts limit hot and humid conditions to a few days. Thunderstorms accompany these airmass changes and several isolated ones can become severe. Expect greater than normal rainfall in the Great Lakes and northern Rockies. The monsoon season arrives farther south with afternoon showers common along the Continental Divide.

AUGUST 2005. The pace of summer weather change slows appreciably this month. Throughout the South, people hearing distant thunder in the late afternoon will not experience rain or high winds — drenching rain comes only under a thunderstorm formation. In the Plains, moisture-laden air from the Gulf of Mexico will flow northward and generate late-afternoon thunderstorms from Oklahoma to the Dakotas. The Rockies and much of Oklahoma will enjoy cool nights after warm days. Afternoon thunderstorms will migrate to the northern reaches of the Continental Divide. The Northeast enjoys seasonable midsummer weather. Several thunderstorms are possible there.

AUTUMN

SEPTEMBER 2005. The remaining effects of El Niño produce subdued hurricane formation in the Atlantic Basin this year. Fewer than normal storms will be named, with only one reaching the criteria for a major hurricane. This will not make a landfall. Frosty weather, early for the season, can be expected in Idaho and Montana, and a dusting of snow will powder the Bitterroots and Tetons in Idaho. The Northeast will also be cooler than normal. Wet weather will produce above-average rainfall in the Mid Atlantic, Ohio Valley and Central Appalachians. Florida will receive its first cool front of the autumn by the 25th. Southern California will be threatened by a rare hurricane which will dissipate before making landfall.

OCTOBER 2005. A steady wind ushers crisp fall air through the Rockies and northern Plains. October is the driest month of the year nationwide, with only a few sparse showers accompanying several cold fronts from the Great Lakes to New England. Fall foliage is especially vivid this year, the result of abundant summer rainfall. The hurricane season ends quietly with only a brief threat to the Gulf States from a tropical storm midmonth. Santa Ana winds are fierce and threatening. Fire endangers residents of southern California. Florida is also dry, with brush fires rampant in the Everglades. A Pacific storm brings gales and windswept rain to Washington and Oregon with a blanket of snow capping the Cascades by the 30th.

NOVEMBER 2005. Shorter days and longer nights bring a chill to all but the South, where evenings are pleasantly cool and dry. Rainfall there is still scarce, though scattered coastal showers will appear on Florida's east coast. Cold air can appear with great suddenness in New England as Arctic air arrives by Thanksgiving. Lake-engendered snow will also fall on western New York State, affecting Rochester, New York and Erie, Pennsylvania. Travel on the New York State Thruway will be hazardous. Pacific Northwest storms are apt to become more numerous, with gale-force winds and majestic coastal waves. Snow will be frequent and heavy in the mountains. The fire danger stays perilous in southern California, preceding the winter rainy season. Chicago receives an early season dusting around the 25th.

WINTER

DECEMBER 2005. Winter's entrance, at first only a whisper, brings flurries to upstate New York and New England early this month. Snowfall is heavier in the West, with Colorado and Utah enjoying a fine early season for skiing. From the Central Great Lakes to the Great Plains the weather is milder than usual, as daily average temperatures are 10 degrees above normal. The area experiences little precipitation. Several storms form just east of the mid-Atlantic States and quickly strengthen. These bring rain to coastal cities and snowfalls averaging 3 to 6 inches west of Interstate 195 as far north as Portland, Maine. A much larger storm impacts this entire region during the last week of the month with the threat of a significant ice storm. Stormy weather is increasing along the West Coast.

JANUARY 2006. Above normal snowfall can be expected from the interior sections of the mid-Atlantic States to New England. In fact, a full-blown blizzard is possible late in the month as a slow-moving ocean storm batters the Northeast. Arctic air during the month brings an icy chill to the Ohio Valley and Great Lakes. Temperatures there are far below normal. Lake effect snowfall remains persistent throughout this region. In Florida, the citrus crop is threatened by frost, though most oranges are harvested before any major damage occurs. The Great Plains enjoy sunny and cold days with several weak storms providing a dusting of snow from Canada. In the Rockies, the storm track brings the heaviest snowfall to the mountains of southern Colorado and northern New Mexico. Heavy snows can also be expected in the central and southern mountains of California with windswept gales along the coast. The Pacific Northwest enjoys unusually dry and cool weather.

FEBRUARY 2006. Winter's snowiest month is highlighted by several slow-moving storms that drop heavy snowfall from Philadelphia to Boston. While these storms will not be particularly powerful, they will last for several days and are capable of producing over a foot of snow. Strong onshore coastal winds through successive high tides will cause some localized damage along shore roads. Temperatures throughout the Midwest and Great Lakes remain below normal as lake effect snowfall ebbs. The Plains remain cool and dry, though a brief tornado outbreak threatens Texas. The mountainous West enjoys excellent winter sports, with fresh powder falling for Colorado and Wyoming skiers at midmonth. After a lull, West Coast storms resume and bring wind and rain farther north, including Washington and Oregon. Florida enjoys sunny and cool weather.

Hans Baldung-Grien   Kaisersperg's *Buch Granatapfel*, 1510

The Seven Deadly Sins

Gregory the Great, pope of the Roman Catholic Church from 590 to 604, may have been the first to define the medieval concept of the Seven Deadly Sins. The pontiff was renowned as a popularizer of ideas often originally pagan: angels, demons, devils, relic worship, miracles, the doctrine of purgatory and the use of allegory. Gregory, later canonized a saint, produced *Dialogues* and *Pastoral* for centuries essential in the education of the clergy.

Piers Plowman, a 14th-century English literary work, gives the Seven human form. Only Pride is feminine. Of the rest, Anger has "two pale eyes, and a sniffling nose" and Greed is "beetle-browed and flabby-lipped, with two bleary eyes." The German artist, Hans Baldung-Grien, depicted them as monsters. The Seven are identified below.

ENGLISH	GERMAN	LATIN
Pride	*Hochfart*	*Superbia*
Envy	*Neid*	*Invidia*
Anger	*Zorn*	*Ira*
Lust	*Unkeuscheit*	*Luxuria*
Greed	*Beitikat*	*Avaritia*
Gluttony	*Fressery*	*Gula*
Sloth	*Tragkait*	*Acedia*

THE EMPEROR'S NEW CLOTHES

MANY YEARS AGO there was an Emperor who was so excessively fond of new clothes that he spent all his money on them. He cared nothing about his soldiers, nor for the theatre, nor for driving in the woods except for the sake of showing off his new clothes. He had a costume for every hour in the day. Instead of saying as one does about any king or emperor, "He is in his council chamber," the people here always said, "The Emperor is in his dressing room."

Life was very gay in the great town where he lived. Hosts of strangers came to visit it every day, and among them were two swindlers. They gave themselves out as weavers and said they knew how to weave the most beautiful fabrics imaginable. Not only were the colors and patterns unusually fine, but the clothes that were made of this cloth had the peculiar quality of becoming invisible to every person who was not fit for the office he held, or who was impossibly dull.

"Those must be splendid clothes," thought the Emperor. "By wearing them I should be able to discover which men in my kingdom are unfitted for their posts. I shall distinguish the wise men from the fools. Yes, I certainly must order some of that stuff to be woven for me."

The Emperor paid the two swindlers a lot of money in advance, so that they might begin their work at once.

They did put up two looms and pretended to weave, but they had nothing whatever upon their shuttles. At the outset they asked for a quantity of the finest silk and the purest gold thread, all of which they put into their own bags while they worked away at the empty looms far into the night.

"I should like to know how those weavers are getting on with their cloth," thought the Emperor, but he felt a little queer when he reflected that anyone who was stupid or unfit for his post would not be able to see it. He certainly thought that he need have no fears for himself, but still he thought he would send somebody else first to see how it was getting on. Everybody in the town knew what wonderful power the stuff possessed, and everyone was anxious to see how stupid his neighbor was.

"I will send my faithful old minister to the weavers," thought the Emperor. "He will be best able to see how the stuff looks, for he is a clever man and no one fulfills his duties better than he does."

So the good old minister went into the room where the two swindlers sat working at the empty loom.

"Heaven help us," thought the old minister, opening his eyes very wide. "Why, I can't see a thing!" But he took care not to say so.

Both the swindlers begged him to be good enough to step a little nearer, and asked if he did not think it a good pattern and beautiful coloring. They pointed to the empty loom. The poor old minister stared as hard as he could, but he could not see anything, for of course there was nothing to see.

"Good heavens," thought he. "Is it possible that I am a fool? I have never thought so, and nobody must know it. Am I not fit for my post? It will never do to say that I cannot see the cloth."

"Well, sir, you don't say anything about the cloth," said the one who was pretending to weave.

"Oh, it is beautiful — quite charming," said the minister, looking through his spectacles. "Such a pattern and such colors! I will certainly tell the Emperor that it pleases me very much."

"We are delighted to hear you say so," said the swindlers, and then they named all the colors and described the peculiar pattern. The old minister paid great attention to what they said, so as to be able to repeat it when he got home to the Emperor.

Then the swindlers went on to demand more money, more silk, and more gold, to be able to proceed with the weaving. But they put it all into their own pockets. Not a single strand was ever put into the loom, but they went on as before, weaving at the empty loom.

The Emperor soon sent another faithful official to see how the cloth was getting on and if it would soon be ready. The same thing happened to him as to the minister. He looked and looked, but as there was only the empty loom, he could see nothing at all.

"Is not this a beautiful piece of cloth?" said both the swindlers, showing and explaining the beautiful pattern and colors which were not there to be seen.

"I know I am no fool," thought the man, "so it must be that I am unfit for my good post. It is very strange, though. However, one must not let it appear so." So he praised the stuff he did not see, and assured the swindlers of his delight in the beautiful colors and originality of design.

"It is absolutely charming," he told the Emperor. Everyone in the town was talking about the splendid fabric.

Now the Emperor thought he would like to see it while it was still on the loom. So, accompanied by a number of selected courtiers, among whom were the two faithful officials who had already seen the imaginary stuff, he went to visit the crafty impostors, who were working away as hard as ever they could at the empty loom.

"It is magnificent," said both the officials. "Only see, Majesty, what a design! What colors!" And they pointed to the empty loom, for they each thought no doubt the others could see the wondrous fabric.

"What?" thought the Emperor. "I see nothing at all. This is terrible! Am I a fool? Am I not fit to be Emperor? Why, nothing worse could happen to me!"

"Oh, it is beautiful," said the Emperor. "It has my highest approval," and he nodded his satisfaction as he gazed at the empty loom. Nothing would induce him to say he could not see anything.

The whole group gazed and gazed, but saw nothing. However, they all exclaimed with his Majesty, "It is very beautiful." And they advised him to wear a suit made of this wonderful cloth on the occasion of a great procession which was about to take place. "Magnificent! Gorgeous! Excellent!" went from mouth to mouth. All were equally delighted with it. The Emperor gave each of the rogues an order of knighthood to be worn in their buttonholes and the title of "Gentleman Weaver."

The swindlers sat up the whole night before the day on which the procession was to take place, burning sixteen candles, so that people might see how anxious they were to get the Emperor's new clothes ready. They pretended to take the stuff off the loom. They cut it out in the air with a huge pair of scissors, and they stitched away with needles without thread.

At last they said, "Now the Emperor's new clothes are ready."

The Emperor with his grandest courtiers went to them himself, and both the swindlers raised one arm in the air, as if they were holding something. They said, "See, these are the trousers.

This is the coat. Here is the mantle," and so on. "It is as light as a spider's web. One might think one had nothing on, but that is the very beauty of it."

"Yes," said all the courtiers, but they could not see anything, for there was nothing to see.

"Will Your Imperial Majesty be graciously pleased to take off your clothes?" said the impostors. "Then we may put on the new ones, along here before the great mirror."

The Emperor took off all his clothes, and the impostors pretended to give him one article of dress after the other. They pretended to fasten something around his waist and to tie on something. This was the train, and the Emperor turned round and round in front of the mirror.

"How well His Majesty looks in the new clothes! How becoming they are!" everyone cried. "What a design, and what colors! They are most gorgeous robes."

"The canopy is waiting outside which is to be carried over Your Majesty in the procession," said the master of the ceremonies.

"Well, I am quite ready," said the Emperor. "Don't the clothes fit well?" Then he turned round again in front of the mirror, so that he should seem to be looking at his grand apparel.

The chamberlains who were to carry the train stooped and pretended to lift it from the ground with both hands, and they walked along with their hands in the air. They dared not let it appear that they could not see anything.

Then the Emperor walked along in the procession under the gorgeous canopy, and everybody in the streets and at the windows exclaimed, "How beautiful are the Emperor's new clothes! What a splendid train! And everything fits to perfection!" Nobody would let it appear that he could see nothing, for then he would not be fit for his post, or else he was a fool.

None of the Emperor's clothes had been so successful before.

"But he has got nothing on," said a little child.

"Oh, listen to the innocent," said his father. And one person whispered to the other what the child had said. "He has nothing on — a child says he has nothing on!"

"But he has nothing on!" at last cried all the people.

The Emperor writhed, for he knew it was true. But he thought, "The procession must go on now." So he held himself stiffer than ever, and the chamberlains held up the invisible train.

— HANS CHRISTIAN ANDERSEN

51

THE SOLAR HOUSES

1. Image
2. Finance
3. Relations
4. Family
5. Children
6. Health
7. Marriage
8. Death
9. Philosophy
10. Fame
11. Friendship
12. Sacrifice

presage

by Dikki-Jo Mullen

ARIES 2005 — PISCES 2006

Think of the night sky. As the Sun sets at the end of the best as well as the worst of days, the night sky awaits, full of beauty and mystery. Astrologers found comfort and counsel offered by the important and highly visible planets Mercury, Venus, Mars, Jupiter, and Saturn as well as the lights or luminaries, the Sun and Moon. Originally, they were linked to the heroic figures of myth. Later, they were analyzed more scientifically as sources of magnetic energy. Then, about three hundred years ago, the outsiders slowly started appearing. Much further away from us and only visible with telescopes, first Uranus, then Neptune, Pluto, and finally Chiron added to the birth chart's message. With each new wanderer (the word planet actually means wanderer), society became more complex.

A planet's discovery allows us to respond to its energies. Major new developments directly related to life on Earth occur when a planet is discovered. During the 1700's Uranus reflected the discovery of electricity and the rise of democracy with the American and French revolutions. During the 1800's Neptune marked the new use of chemicals, conquest of the sea, and the rise of psy-chology and spiritualism. In 1930 Pluto's discovery coincided with the onset of the Atomic Age and mass population growth. In 1977 Chiron was linked to new frontiers of the mind being opened through computer technology.

The remote wilderness of the solar system, edging deep space, has just dealt astrologers yet another wild card. Over the past year a tenth rock from the Sun, the planet Sedna, has been discovered. The Wheel of Fortune can be expected to spin again as this ultimate outsider expresses its message.

During the coming year, Saturn begins a passage in Leo on July 17, linking the Sun and a fire sign with Earth. Mars takes a very long tour through Taurus, from July 28–February 17. Passionate determination is a keynote for these powerful transits. The eclipse pattern is flavored primarily by Aries, the first fire sign of spring. Read all about what these and the other celestial cycles mean to you in Presage. Consider the forecasts for your Moon and ascendant signs as well as the familiar Sun or birth sign for a more detailed astrological overview of your year to come.

ASTROLOGICAL KEYS

Signs of the Zodiac
Channels of Expression

ARIES: pioneer, leader, competitor
TAURUS: earthy, stable, practical
GEMINI: dual, lively, versatile
CANCER: protective, traditional
LEO: dramatic, flamboyant, warm
VIRGO: conscientious, analytical
LIBRA: refined, fair, sociable
SCORPIO: intense, secretive, ambitious
SAGITTARIUS: friendly, expansive
CAPRICORN: cautious, materialistic
AQUARIUS: inquisitive, unpredictable
PISCES: responsive, dependent, fanciful

Elements

FIRE: Aries, Leo, Sagittarius
EARTH: Taurus, Virgo, Capricorn
AIR: Gemini, Libra, Aquarius
WATER: Cancer, Scorpio, Pisces

Qualities

CARDINAL	FIXED	MUTABLE
Aries	Taurus	Gemini
Cancer	Leo	Virgo
Libra	Scorpio	Sagittarius
Capricorn	Aquarius	Pisces

CARDINAL signs mark the beginning of each new season — active.
FIXED signs represent the season at its height — steadfast.
MUTABLE signs herald a change of season — variable.

Celestial Bodies
Generating Energy of the Cosmos

Sun: birth sign, ego, identity
Moon: emotions, memories, personality
Mercury: communication, intellect, skills
Venus: love, pleasures, the fine arts
Mars: energy, challenges, sports
Jupiter: expansion, religion, happiness
Saturn: responsibility, maturity, realities
Uranus: originality, science, progress
Neptune: dreams, illusions, inspiration
Pluto: rebirth, renewal, resources

Glossary of Aspects

Conjunction: two planets within the same sign or less than 10 degrees apart, favorable or unfavorable according to the nature of the planets.

Sextile: a pleasant, harmonious aspect occurring when two planets are two signs or 60 degrees apart.

Square: a major negative effect resulting when planets are three signs from one another or 90 degrees apart.

Trine: planets four signs or 120 degrees apart, forming a positive and favorable influence.

Quincunx: a mildly negative aspect produced when planets are five signs or 150 degrees apart.

Opposition: a six sign or 180 degrees separation of planets generating positive or negative forces depending on the planets involved.

The Houses — *Twelve Areas of Life*

1st house: appearance, image, identity
2nd house: money, possessions, tools
3rd house: communications, siblings
4th house: family, domesticity, security
5th house: romance, creativity, children
6th house: daily routine, service, health
7th house: marriage, partnerships, union
8th house: passion, death, rebirth, soul
9th house: travel, philosophy, education
10th house: fame, achievement, mastery
11th house: goals, friends, high hopes
12th house: sacrifice, solitude, privacy

ECLIPSES

The aura of an eclipse suggests excitement. When the light of one celestial body is blocked by another, changes and the unexpected are afoot. The heavenly body which is shadowed (usually the Sun or Moon) has its energy redirected in the astrological chart. From the darkness following that brief extinguishing of the light springs the promise of new ideas. Potential and birth are the keynotes of an eclipse pattern. Conjunctions to the nodes of the Moon determine the occurrence and totality of solar and lunar eclipses. (Nodes are the intersection points between the Moon's orbit and the plane of the ecliptic.) The north node nurtures and gives while the south node demands and drains. Therefore, eclipses conjunct the north node of the Moon are thought to be more favorable than the eclipses conjunct the south node. Rituals and meditations conducted during eclipses have a special potency, especially if any type of change is the desired goal.

When an eclipse is within three degrees of a planet in the birth chart it will stir the latent potentials of that planet. The most powerful impacts occur when the eclipse is within three days of the birthday, for this shows a conjunction with the natal Sun. Solar eclipses always occur at the New Moon with the Sun and Moon in the same sign. Lunar eclipses take place with the Full Moon as the Sun and Moon oppose each other positioned exactly across the zodiac.

April 8	New Moon Solar in Aries, north node
April 24	Full Moon Lunar in Scorpio, south node
October 3	New Moon Solar in Libra, south node
October 17	Full Moon Lunar in Aries, north node
March 14	Full Moon Lunar in Virgo, south node

PLANETS IN RETROGRADE MOTION

When it is retrograde, a planet appears to be moving backwards. Actually, this is an optical illusion created by its rate of travel relative to Earth's motion. However, illusion or not, the impact is one that changes all of the usual rules. Awareness of repeating patterns is important in making needed changes. Retrogrades mark times when a second chance is offered.

Mercury turns retrograde more often than any other planet. For about three weeks three or four times a year it will delay travel, scramble communication, and bring back old acquaintances. It is a good time to stay in familiar places and to tie up loose ends.

Here are the upcoming Mercury retrograde cycles:

March 20 — April 13
in Aries

July 23 — August 16
in Leo

November 15 — December 4
in Scorpio and Sagittarius

March 3 — 26
in Pisces and Aries

Venus turns retrograde less frequently than any other planet. When this does take place it's best to be patient regarding matters of the heart. Manage finances with discretion and shop for the best price. It's not the time to risk an impulsive expenditure. Venus will be retrograde in Capricorn and Aquarius December 26–February 4.

A Mars retrograde is significant regarding conflict. Aggression is not rewarded with victory. It's best to be subtle and use strategy in coping with adversaries. Military situations take unexpected turns. Competitions are prone to upsets. Mechanical and electrical items require repair or replacement. Mars will be retrograde in Taurus October 2–December 10.

ARIES

The year ahead for those
born under the sign of the Ram
March 21–April 20

As the celestial trailblazer you, Aries, are spring's herald. All that is fresh and fiery and progressive is in harmony with the Ram. Gifted with great energy from ruling planet Mars, Aries is a restless pacesetter. Courage is one of your defining traits. So is an ardent desire for progress and a forward leap. Directing these energies wisely is the real challenge. Wild and impetuous, it is essential that you make time for reflection and self-examination.

Mercury teeters, pauses, then turns retrograde in your birth sign exactly on the vernal equinox. Review studies and complete projects through your birthday. You can solve problems and clear away debris. The Aries solar eclipse on April 8 accents endings and beginnings. It's a time of surprise. Be receptive to the changes, and this will be a pleasantly memorable year. Late April through Beltane is a perfect time to hit the road. Celebrate May Eve hiking or writing poetry among the flowers. There will be a yearning for solitude from the beginning of May through June 11 as Mars is buried in your 12th house. As the summer solstice nears, Mars crosses into your sign, and motivation returns. Quell anger or impatience though.

Mercury and Venus waltz together in Leo, through your 5th house of love and pleasure, during most of July. On July 17 Saturn shifts into Leo and forms a trio with them. This sets the stage for serious commitments and a cycle of meaningful creativity. The New Moon after Lammas,

on August 4, brings a burst of artistic energy. A new hobby or project can be shared with one you love and admire. From mid-August until just before Mabon, on September 23, Venus joins Jupiter in Libra. This friendly air sign pattern brings teamwork and cooperation to assure success. Charming and talented associates create opportunities for you to fulfill a cherished wish. The magic inherent in color, music, and art can deepen your spiritual work. Try balancing your chakras with color and sound.

Legal matters can be concluded successfully in early September. Listen and concentrate during the first week of October. Both Mercury and the Sun will oppose you, creating some distractions and preoccupation. On October 17 the Full Moon brings another eclipse in your sign. Transformations which began in the springtime will reach new potentials. Life is full of sparkle, but resist the temptation to control. Recognize and respect synchronicity. Allow destiny to play her hand and you will triumph eventually. At All Hallows Mercury begins a long passage through your travel sector. Journeys of the mind as well as actual geographical wanderings will take you to new places during late autumn. New concepts can broaden your outlook.

Just after Yule Venus will retrograde between your 10th and 11th houses. Friendships can impact career. Be aware of cycles and patterns in your social life. As 2005 draws to a close, past life connections will become apparent in intimate relationships. From early January through Candlemas the heavens accent the Earth signs. Capricorn placements dominate your 10th house, squaring your Sun. You will be highly visible at work. Expect some competitive situations. Take time off to care for your home and enjoy family life during the week of January 14, though. The Full Moon in Cancer at that time heightens your devotion to relatives or your extended family and illuminates the important roles they play in your life. Devote magical workings to career goals or job politics at Candlemas sabbat. On February 9 Mercury joins Uranus in Pisces in your 12th house. You're more introspective than usual. Dream activity accelerates. Try keeping a journal as an aid in understanding your personal motivations. Solitary meditations and rituals will be quite effective.

In winter's final days, after March 6, Venus will join Neptune to favorably sextile your Sun from the 11th house. Friendships will offer new opportunity. Creative projects, including musical studies, will provide a catalyst in selecting long-term goals. It will be especially easy for you to read others psychically. Experiment with aura gazing and telepathy. Be aware of clocks, watches, and calendars. Time keepers are helpful friends in disguise. Mars' position will clash with Mercury's retrograde in Pisces during March. If a vehicle needs replacement, start to examine your options promptly. Verify departure times and reservations; there can be some last minute schedule changes to allow for. The weather may impact you, so have dry, comfortable clothing available, especially footwear.

HEALTH

With eclipses in your birth sign on April 8 and October 17 it is important to be aware of changes in vitality. Care for your teeth and mouth as a route to overall wellness this year. Create healthy attitudes about finances and maintain relaxed working conditions while Mars is retrograde in your 2nd house of security and earnings from October 2–December 9. Add fresh apples to your diet. The old adage "an apple a day keeps the doctor away" applies to you now.

LOVE

The earliest days of spring find romantic Venus making a curtsey in your sign. Your beauty and desirability will be at a peak from the vernal equinox through April 15. At the same time an eclipse pattern lends a note of instability. Cope by approaching new relationships with caution. At the same time be honest about ending liaisons that are no longer serving a purpose. Plan a flamboyant Independence Day party

followed by a summer vacation with someone you love during July. Favorable fire sign transits in your love and pleasure sector during the longest and brightest days of summer promise deep joy. Try the Feng Shui treatment of using peach-colored sheets on your bed to sweeten and brighten love connections during July and August.

SPIRITUALITY

Pluto hovers in your 9th house of philosophy and the higher mind all year. Examine beliefs about the afterlife and the survival of the spirit. The more genteel and romantic vampire and werewolf legends can provide encoded messages about the denizens of other planes. Walk in the light of the Full Moon on May 23-24 to experience the deeper messages of this trend. That particular lunation will be in a wide conjunction with Pluto. All the year long resist the temptation to adamantly share your beliefs with those who really are not receptive. Respect spiritual doctrines you don't personally approve of at present.

FINANCE

From late July until February 17 Mars will transit your 2nd house of finances and earning power, motivating you to work especially hard during that time. Enthusiasm to add to your income is at an all-time peak. However, be careful not to overwork. Peace of mind, rest, and wellness must not be sacrificed for material security. Control any anger about money matters. Direct this tremendous energy into finding constructive solutions instead. Jupiter opposes you from the spring until just before Samhain. Well-meaning advisors or promoters can offer you the wrong advice. If in doubt, follow your own instincts. Resist influence of another's ideas. Postpone entering into any business partnerships this year until after October 25. If others seek your financial assistance, provide them with encouragement and ideas rather than a loan. A tax return, insurance settlement, inheritance, or the rewards from an investment could add nicely to your financial security between November and early March.

TAURUS

The year ahead for those
born under the sign of the Bull
April 21–May 21

Tremendously persistent, yet affectionate, the Bull represents the premier Earth energy. Natural beauty and creature comforts are the delight of Venus-ruled Taurus. Green, growing things respond with love to the touch of this sign, which belongs to some of the zodiac's best gardeners. Uncanny insight and intuition is often a Taurus trait. In Egypt the black and white bull named Apis was honored with offerings of coins and fragrant oils in order to procure a vision of the future. An emblem of art, wealth, and music, the celestial bull accepts only the best of earthly goods. Those who refuse to accept less than the best will often receive it.

Spring begins with Mars leaping over the midheaven of your birth chart. It will remain in your 10th house until May Eve. Career matters are of prime concern. Your deep devotion leads you above and beyond the call of duty now. A little humor and perspective are a must. Otherwise, the intensity of your feelings could overwhelm professional associates. On April 16 Venus enters your sign, where it will remain until May 9. Love and appreciation for all that you do and are will be given freely. Since Taurus links especially to sound, enjoy ritual music. The Taurus New Moon on May 8 is especially wonderful for magical practices involving bells, whistles, flutes, and other instruments. During much of the last half of May Mercury moves rapidly through Taurus in a harmonious sextile aspect to

planets in Cancer and Pisces. Discussions and written messages can produce many good works. Travel will be more rewarding than expected; proceed confidently with journeys of all kinds.

Early June finds Jupiter changing direction in your 6th house. Animal companions heal and comfort. At the same time, make certain that cherished critters are current on their shots and veterinary checkups. A new animal companion might join you. Near Midsummer Day the love and advice of a neighbor or sibling can make a difference for the better. During mid-July make your dwelling a comfortable sanctuary. It's the time to begin home improvements, as both Venus and Mars highlight the home and family sector. Mars begins a very long passage through your sign as July ends. This will last until after Valentine's Day. You'll have tremendous energy and motivation, but could be quick to anger. Focus on only constructive thoughts and actions and the world will be at your feet. Venus aspects Mars with a romantic trine near Lammas Eve. Romance is in full flower, as your pleasure and love sector is accented by these cosmic sweethearts. String rose quartz and turquoise beads to create a love charm rosary. During the last half of August beneficial Libra transits highlight good health and vitality. Aromatherapy and home remedies suggested by friends can help.

In early September Mercury moves into a trine with your Sun. Enroll in classes, order books, and catch up on correspondence. If you've always wanted to write, this is the time to give it a try. At the autumn equinox Venus moves into an opposition aspect. In the weeks following this your closest relationships will require some effort. The secret to maintaining harmony is to try to see both sides. Be a very good listener. Avoid legal entanglements in early October. At Samhain Pluto, Mercury, and Venus will cluster in your 8th house. The veil to the afterlife will be especially transparent. Spirit guides and loved ones on the other side can communicate quite clearly. The Full Moon on November 15 in your sign is strongly aspected by several fixed sign planets including Mars. Near that date be flexible and objective. Important matters demand attention. Make your best effort; others expect much of you.

November finds Jupiter beginning a long passage through your relationship sector. A spouse or partner is about to become more successful. Allow them to grow; offer encouragement. Legal issues take a turn for the better before Yule. Your ruler, Venus, is retrograde December 26–February 4. Kindness and patience are needed. Romantic involvements and friendships are subject to special stresses then. Don't overextend financially in early 2006. Hunt for bargains at post Yuletide sales. At Candlemas focus on rituals of release and forgiveness. After February 9 Mercury will be in Pisces. The head and heart will be in harmony. You will be able to formulate good goals and make the best choices at mid-month. Friends provide help and guidance. At the end of February the planetary warrior, Mars, leaves Taurus. The last days of winter will find you more relaxed than you have been for many months. Pleasant greeting cards, jokes, or thoughtful telephone calls will improve all kinds of exchanges. Communicate creatively. Compose a rhyme.

HEALTH

Your sweet tooth is legendary. Desserts and rich foods can be almost irresistible. The secret is to savor very small portions of that delectable chocolate cheesecake and lemon meringue pie. Stress can be a major health factor from July to February when Mars is in your sign. Do not overdo physical activity then. Get in shape gradually. Avoid extreme heat. A retrograde Venus from just after Yule through Candlemas says watch health habits. Your heredity can also provide clues to fitness factors late in the year.

LOVE

With mercurial Virgo ruling your romance sector, retrograde Mercury patterns usually will provide opportunities to rekindle old flames. Taurus often prefers the tried and true and prefers not to let go. If you are inclined to take a second chance at an old love, March 20–April 13, July 23–August 16, and November 15–December 4 are the times to give it another try. Frequent a spa, health club, or gym to make new love contacts. The lunar eclipse of March 14 promises profound revelations, upsets, sparkles, and surprises linked directly to matters of the heart as the winter wanes. Wait until after that to try a deep commitment. Your truest romantic wishes are undergoing a metamorphosis. Watch for butterfly omens in order to understand the specifics.

SPIRITUALITY

Mystical Neptune hovers near your 10th house of fame and fortune all year. Finding spiritual fulfillment in your work is possible. Seek ways to apply spiritual truths to your profession. If you are dissatisfied with your career, a time of contemplation at a sacred site could provide answers. Make time for some yoga and meditation sessions on your lunch hour. Create a small journal filled with written affirmations. This should help in your quest to combine worldly successes with spiritual enhancement and awakening.

FINANCE

Pluto's influence in your 8th house is making you especially aware of how worldwide economic factors can impact your personal finances. After July 18 Saturn will enter your 4th house of residence and relatives. Find affordable housing. A family member may turn to you for a loan or financial advice around mid-July. Reply with tact and kindness. Taureans tend to manage the finances of the family and business associates. Partners will encourage you to expand in business matters and seek a more opulent standard of living after October 26. Trust your own instincts. On that day Jupiter commences a year-long transit through your 7th house of relationships. Teamwork begins to bless your personal security. A role model can inspire you in regard to your financial achievements.

GEMINI

The year ahead for those
born under the sign of the Twins
May 22–June 21

The scepter carried by the winged messenger Mercury, planetary ruler of Gemini, is formed from two intertwined serpents. Called the caduceus, this celestial walking staff blends nature's duality and places it in useful harmony. Male and female, light and dark, ascending and descending, the Twins are walkers on the wind. Gemini is concerned with channeling words, thoughts, and ideas. Conversation, teaching, and media coverage are all linked to the zodiacal twins. The Twins came to Europe through Asian legends about brothers named Gorgos (Mad George) and Myakka (Knight Michael). George the jester and Michael, the good soldier, dragon slayer, and healer eventually changed roles, became saints and had their symbols incorporated into Britain's banner, the Union Jack.

Spring's first dawn hints at memories as Mercury begins the year in retrograde motion. The eclipse on April 8 will bring revelations concerning a close friend. Through mid-April there is time to reconsider the value of longtime associates and old goals. Learn from the past, then release it. On April 13 a more progressive trend begins. A trine from Mars and Neptune in your brother air sign of Aquarius generates enthusiasm for the food, music, and languages of other lands as Beltane nears. Opportunities to make pilgrimages to spiritual sites are possible now. It's also the perfect time to become more involved in higher education. During May, Venus, the Sun, and Mercury all tour your 12th

house. Deep peace and satisfaction come through time spent in solitary reverie. Quiet good deeds and kindnesses performed will deepen your personal happiness. Expect to notice a stronger rapport with wild places. Through early June Mercury moves rapidly through your sign. Problems can be solved and decisions made. The Gemini New Moon on June 6 corresponds with Jupiter turning direct in Libra. The love and pleasure sector is impacted. Your personality can open new doors. Express creativity. A new romantic interest or an enjoyable new avocation will brighten your birthday month. Instinctively you will say and do all of the right things to increase trust and bonding with children during mid-June.

At the summer solstice the focus shifts to financial security. Venus, Mercury, the Sun, and Saturn will all cluster in your 2nd house of finances. Earning enough to pay for new treasures will absorb your attention. Enjoy all that you have, rather than lamenting that which eludes. If you must travel during July, do so before the 16th. After that Saturn, followed by a retrograde Mercury, will create some turbulence in your 3rd house. Vehicles can be unreliable or directions lost. Celebrate Lammas in familiar surroundings. Use care in communication during this time, for messages can be lost or misconstrued. Carrying a talisman of citrine for clarity can be most helpful. Burn gum copal combined with mint leaves over charcoal for a centering spell. The mental cobwebs will be swept away and you'll find your path again.

The first half of August finds Venus in your 4th house of home and family life. Family dynamics will be especially upbeat. The remainder of August brings Jupiter and Venus together in Libra creating perfect aspects to your Sun for a climate of romance. The Full Moon in Aquarius on August 19 will illuminate all of the joyful potentials of this trend. For some Geminians it will strongly favor the birth of a child. For others, creative expression or the flowering of romance will occur. During summer's last golden weeks a mutable T-square with Pisces, Virgo, and Sagittarius transits reminds you to focus on business.

A more competitive trend builds. With the autumn equinox, favorable aspects to your Sun combined with Venus moving into your health sector promise increased vitality. The Octber eclipses could upset the status quo regarding romance and friendship. An old love or dream may be discarded suddenly. At All Hallows Mercury begins a long passage through your opposing sign of Sagittarius. Others will make suggestions and issue invitations all the way through Yuletide. Read between the lines. There is much to learn through listening and observing.

The gloom time finds retrograde Mars buried deeply in your 12th house. Find an outlet for repressed anger. Strategy will appeal to you. Look at the Full Moon on December 15. It falls in your sign and carries a personal message about reaching your higher self. Expect a breakthrough in completing an ongoing project at the lunation. January begins with several Capricorn placements in your 8th house, including Mercury. There can be some research to complete. The week before Candlemas Mercury moves into a conjunction with Neptune. Both planets make a positive trine aspect to your Sun. Psychic insights are vivid. Try crystal gazing or set out the Tarot cards. Keep a notebook handy to jot down impressions. Your mind is working overtime. Mars enters Gemini on February 18 where it will remain through the remainder of the winter. A tidal wave of energy seems to engulf you. Projects you've postponed suddenly can't wait. Control angry impulses. Be constructive and pro-active instead. Exercise provides the perfect outlet and mood balancer.

HEALTH

Pluto rules your health sector. The health of others has directly impacted your personal wellness for many years because Pluto has been transiting in an opposition from your 7th house of relationships. Take precautions if you're in direct contact with those who are ill or who create stress in your life. Since Gemini has a rulership over the hands and arms, experiment with using handheld Chinese exercise balls. Also mastering some yoga mudra hand gestures can be helpful. Massage the hands and arms with fragrant oils or lotions and the health of your entire body will be enhanced.

LOVE

Benevolent Jupiter brightens your 5th house of romance from the vernal equinox until just before Hallowmas. A really nurturing and promising relationship is likely to become a part of your life then. From May 10–June 3 and August 18–September 10 Venus will complement Jupiter with trine and conjunction aspects, respectively. Those weeks are especially good for either investing in an existing relationship or seeking a new love. Since artistic Libra rules love in your birth chart, try attending concerts and art gallery openings or enrolling in art classes.

SPIRITUALITY

Springtime finds Mars conjoining Neptune in Aquarius impacting your 9th house of spirituality and philosophy. This is an icy and winter-like energy. It's ideal for exploring Scandinavian mystical practices in the form of rune lore. Chant the names of runes. Select one at random, then inscribe it on a sea shell or wooden tablet with marking pens. Carry it with you as talisman. To try runic yoga, pose your body in postures that suggest the actual physical appearance of runes. Become one with the runes.

FINANCE

Stern Saturn has been in your financial sector for the past couple of years. You've been concerned about security. This trend will ebb on July 17 when Saturn changes signs. In anticipation, dedicate the Litha sabbat to prosperity. Light a green candle just as summer begins and purchase a beautiful basil plant. Nurture the basil with love, sun, and water until the autumn harvest time. After Lammas, as the spell's power builds, your financial picture should grow promising. October's eclipse pattern indicates that a creative idea or hobby could turn into a profit-making venture.

CANCER

The year ahead for those
born under the sign of the Crab
June 22–July 23

A sensitive and vulnerable being dwells behind the hard exterior shell of the Crab. Carrying its home wherever it wanders, the silent Crab exudes caution and patience. Whether she was an angel or a demon, the mother figure is the most important person in the life of the Moonchild. This gracious and kindly water sign also has been represented by a turtle and a sacred scarab beetle. Among the Chaldeans the constellation Cancer was a heavenly doorway called "The Gate of Men." It was the path which led to the Earth and birth. Again, the link to the mother is underscored.

Longtime friendships and old loves generate a comforting warmth during the first chilly days of spring. A Venus transit in the last degrees of Pisces creates a stabilizing support system. The good people in your life bring special blessings. Saturn completes its retrograde on March 22 and moves rapidly through your sign until July 16, setting the mood for the spring and early summer. It's a pattern that has made the last two years something of a reality check. Keep working, and be conscientious. The rewards are just around the corner. A serious state of mind prevails. You are juggling to balance domestic and professional responsibilities. The eclipse of April 8 is a significant one, marking a new cycle at work. You could begin a new career. Accept changes gracefully in regard to your professional situation. Write a list of desired goals and affirmations and dedicate it to the New Moon on the 8th. Read the list daily during the next month. On May Eve Mars will enter Pisces, your sister water sign. This helps your physical vitality and enables you to deal with old conflicts and frustrations with aplomb. This upbeat influence will last through June 11. The healing and energizing qualities of water will be especially powerful during this entire period. Take time to walk by the sea or in the rain. Add herbs and essences to bath water. Bless sacred water for ritual work. From June 4-28 Venus will smile as she dances through your sign, Mercury joins the happy parade on June 12. Love and involvement in the fine arts bring joy this month. Accept invitations near Midsummer Eve. Take a vacation or finalize future travel plans. A visit to a childhood friend or relative who has been out of touch can set the scene for a magical respite.

A New Moon in Cancer on July 6 is accompanied by a variety of fire sign transits. Security issues are accented. You'll feel the need to work hard to assure material comforts. After your birthday, any anger linked to work issues or past sacrifices you've made will lessen. Mars and Saturn will both exit cardinal signs, so the pressure is released. Postpone financial decisions until August 16. Mercury will turn direct in your money sector and your judgment about practical matters will be clearer. During late August and September Venus will join Jupiter in the 4th house. These two benefic planets in the sector of residence and real estate can bring some wonderful opportunities to acquire a larger, more comfortable dwelling. Shop for items you especially would like to have in your home. October's eclipse pattern could find you planning a residential move.

At All Hallows Eve Mercury will join Venus and Pluto in Sagittarius, your 6th house. Memories of a childhood animal companion can be especially poignant. A charitable donation to animal charities would be a great way to acknowledge the sabbat. You could be rewarded with a dreamtime visit from animal spirits. The retrograde Mercury of November 15 – December 4 is a good time to get organized. Complete projects which have been in progress too long. Past health history or heredity can provide clues concerning health decisions near Thanksgiving. Just before Yule, Mars completes its retrograde in Taurus, your 11th house. A friend has reason to celebrate an accomplishment. Offer a meaningful token in honor of the occasion.

December favors membership in groups and organizations. Companionship can be healing and inspirational as 2005 closes. The Full Moon on January 14 falls in your sign, opposing both Mercury and Venus. Be a good listener; compromise if any differences arise. Mirrors can be especially wonderful tools in meditation and ritual. Gaze at the Full Moon's face in a favorite mirror. Record the impressions received in your Book of Shadows for future reference. Near Candlemas Mars and Jupiter will strongly aspect each other in your 11th and 5th houses. Adventurous leisure time activities and hobbies will have allure. Be gentle and thoughtful with those you love. This pattern creates conflicts of interest involving someone close to you. On February 9 Mercury begins a long passage through Pisces which will last the rest of the winter. Your 9th house is blessed by this. Communication and understanding will be greatly improved. The last weeks of winter favor both study and travel. You can touch the hearts of others with your eloquent writing and speaking then.

HEALTH

Saturn has been moving slowly through your sign for two years. After its exit in July, your vitality should improve. Just before All Hallows, healing Jupiter enters Scorpio for a year-long passage and creates a favorable trine aspect to your Sun. Health matters should improve steadily during the last half of the year. Since water signs are involved, season food with sea salt and drink plenty of liquids to speed the healing process. Cut down on caffeine and hot spices. Your sensitive system can overreact to the stimulation otherwise.

LOVE

The eclipse at the Full Moon in Scorpio on April 24 falls directly in your sector of love and romance. An eclipse promises a shake-up. There can be new interests and discoveries linked to a current relationship. If a tie has outlived its usefulness, this is a time to let go and move forward. Devote the Beltane sabbat to love magic. Weave a heart charm of lace and ribbon and present it to someone you've admired from afar. When the prettiest of May's flowers bloom, love should beckon back.

SPIRITUALITY

Uranus, ruler of astrology, sizzles in your spiritual sector all year. Different zodiac systems and symbols from around the world can provide a marvelous spiritual catalyst. Study the Nazca zodiac of Peru, the Egyptian zodiac, Native American medicine wheel, or the Celtic tree alphabet. The Full Moon in Pisces on September 17 conjoins Uranus and ushers in a potent four-week cycle of spiritual awakening. Research the mythology surrounding the Crab, your familiar emblem, for further insight.

FINANCE

With Leo ruling your financial sector, you take great pride in managing finances with honesty and dignity. Saturn will begin a long passage through your money house in July. Accept financial parameters gracefully after your birthday. Work hard to improve your salable job skills. The rewards will start to come in when Jupiter enters Scorpio in late October. From autumn through winter this positive transit will create a trine to Uranus in Pisces, pointing to wish fulfillment and enhanced wealth. A money charm created from antique coins could be very effective. Assemble one on a Thursday or a Monday while the Moon waxes.

LEO

The year ahead for those
born under the sign of the Lion
July 24–August 23

Identified with the Sun, Leo is synonymous with royalty. Blending confidence with affection, the Lion shines with genuine charisma. In Egypt the Lion was worshipped as Sekhmet, a fire goddess who offered passage to the underworld. In Babylon the divine Ishtar rode in a chariot drawn by seven lions. Alchemists in medieval times used lion emblems to illustrate the powerful potentials in chemical processes. A similar alchemy is in evidence when a Leo is encouraged by sincere compliments. Great things tend to happen.

With the vernal equinox Mars joins Neptune in Aquarius, your opposing sign. Don't take others for granted; associates might not be as they first appear. Competitive situations are present through the end of April. If you are the winner in a conflict, be alert to the possibility of reprisals or poor sportsmanship. On May Eve, Mercury in Aries moves toward a trine with Pluto in Sagittarius. This favorable pattern involving both of the other fire signs culminates at the New Moon on May 8. Clashes will be resolved amicably. There could be some recognition at work, as your 10th house is involved. Through the rest of May until June 3, Venus creates harmony with friends. Your 11th house benefits from a sextile aspect. Follow through with networking; blend business and pleasure.

As the summer solstice approaches several planets, including Saturn, gather in your 12th house. You'll be alone more than usual. Use this time wisely. There's so much that can be accomplished. By June 29 both Mercury and Venus will be in Leo and your 1st house where they'll trine Mars in fiery Aries. Through late July your personality and appearance impress others. Perfect your ability in a sport, audition for a role in community theater, or take a special trip. On July 23 Mercury turns retrograde in your sign. You can acquire deeper understanding of an important subject. Review notes and reread significant books. The New Moon on August 4 in your sign brings awareness of your strengths and weaknesses. Saturn begins a long passage through Leo just before your birthday, ushering in a more serious pattern. All will be well if you work hard and consider practical needs. Patience is always helpful when Saturn is powerful. Plan time and schedules carefully.

During the last half of August through early September, Venus adds charm and creativity to your 3rd house. Your communication ability will be top-notch, so use it. A relationship with a neighbor or sibling improves. At the autumn equinox five planets in fixed signs make powerful aspects to your Sun. Much is expected of you. Identify priorities and get plenty of rest. The eclipses on October 3 and 17 are very beneficial for you. They promise greater freedom and positive change, especially regarding love situations and long-range goals. Cultivate new friendships. On Halloween Mercury will begin a friendly passage through Sagittarius, a kindred fire sign. Celebrate with a focus on fire magic. During November the Sun and Jupiter in your 4th house bring growth linked to home and family life. Relatives can be entering new life stages, or a residence may need updating. Be flexible. November 27–December 12 finds Mercury at a station in the 4th house. Conversations with and about relatives are revealing. Visitors arriving after Thanksgiving offer valuable input. You might feel the need to change the status quo at home again. The noise level at home can be a factor.

At the winter solstice Aquarius transits involving Neptune and Venus move into your relationship sector. Brush away illusions regarding love and commitment. A dream offers surprising new insights about a relationship. On December 30 stay comfortable and get plenty of rest. The New Moon that day can mark a lower physical energy. As 2006 begins Capricorn placements accent your 6th house of health. Since Mercury is involved, be aware of how your mindset can affect wellness. Gather information related to health. Through Candlemas week Venus will be retrograde in the health sector. Don't let friends offer you foods or beverages you know aren't healthy choices. The February 13 Full Moon in Leo makes this an emotional Valentine's Eve. Your sign has a traditional link with the heart. Offer a heart-shaped trinket or treat to the one you care for.

Uranus and Mercury are joined by the Sun in your 8th house from February 19 on. There can be an interest in near-death experiences, reincarnation, or communication with the spirit world. A sudden shift in your long-held perception about these matters is likely. The time period from the Pisces New Moon on February 27 to the eclipse of March 14 can be pivotal regarding this. Winter concludes with Mars in Gemini activating your 11th house. New challenges are attractive. A friend's enthusiasm for change encourages you to be more adventurous.

HEALTH
Saturn rules health in your chart. In July this heavenly heavyweight will begin a long passage through your sign. Patience with reaching health goals is essential. Wellness is achieved through sustained effort right now. A few hours of extra sleep now and then is the best gift you can give yourself this year. Be especially careful to avoid too much exposure to the sun, inclement weather, and wind. Purchase a safari hat and a really good umbrella as birthday gifts to yourself.

LOVE
Free-spirited, idealistic Sagittarius rules your 5th house of love. The Full Moon on May 23 impacts that area of the birth chart, ushering in a four-week cycle when you'll be noticed and sought after. Venus passes through Leo from June 29–July 23. Circulate, work at cementing bonds, and by your birthday closest love connections can deepen in a wonderful way. Make certain that you enjoy the animals cherished by someone you love and vice-versa. If trying a love spell, always include your cat or other familiar in the ritual process. Take note of how your favorite animal reacts to a new love. That insight can prove valuable.

SPIRITUALITY
There are two eclipses in your 9th house this year, on April 8 and October 17. This promises a whole new meaning to philosophical concepts and spirituality before Samhain. A familiar belief system may be released in favor of new perspectives. Spiritual books and recordings can be especially helpful now. Be open to new experience. A visit to a sacred site such as a Native American mound, Buddhist temple, or go abroad to see Stonehenge, Delphi or Carnac. Any of these could be the catalyst for profound spiritual awakening. When Jupiter enters your 4th house in October a favorable cycle for hosting a meditation group, coven meeting, or a séance circle in your own home commences.

FINANCE
The March 14 eclipse falls directly in your 2nd house of cash flow. A source of income could either disappear or generate new needs. Change in the world as a whole may impact your field. Saturn's entry into Leo right before your birthday promises a need for your services but also accents the work ethic. Rewards come to those who work hard. Saturn relates to time. This year would be an optimum time to emulate feng shui practitioners who often place an octagon or oval clock in the workplace to symbolize forward motion. Golden and bright green candles burned regularly would create a simple but effective prosperity ritual.

VIRGO

*The year ahead for those
born under the sign of the Virgin*
August 24–September 23

The maiden holding a sheaf of newly harvested grain shows at first glance Virgo's link with the Earth and the tangible rewards of service. A closer inspection reveals she is also depicted with hints of wings and a halo, lending the purity and agility of winged Mercury, her ruling planet. The maiden is the Greek goddess Hygeia, who has given her name to the science of hygiene. She appears again as Vesta, the Roman goddess of purity, a sister who patiently tends the everlasting flame. Discriminating, meticulous, and analytical are Virgo's identifying traits.

The vernal equinox opens an old door, for Mercury turns retrograde in your 8th house just as spring begins. A riddle is answered or a secret revealed, bringing a sense of closure. Be aware of the financial patterns of a partner. If your security has been threatened before by the choices of another, take care not to let it happen again. Examine financial documents with special care before signing through April 13. Late April through Beltane finds Venus in Taurus making a wonderful aspect to your Sun. Music brings inspiration under this trend. The prospects are very bright for making love connections. This is especially true if you're traveling. During the last half of May Mercury moves rapidly through your 9th house. Note current events; gather books and other reference materials. There is much to learn. Foreign language skills come easily now. Creative word usage will impart a special power to magical workings.

The Gemini New Moon on June 6 in your fame and fortune sector will trine Jupiter as it turns direct in your 2nd house of finances. This is very promising for recognition, a promotion, or an opportunity for added income by the summer solstice. Late June finds Mercury, Venus, and Saturn close together in the last degrees of Cancer. This could involve you in politics. It favors group projects and community service. After Independence Day, July finds you growing more introspective. Leo transits, including Saturn, are moving over the 12th house cusp. Use visualization to find inner peace. July 23 is an interesting day, as Venus enters your sign and Mercury turns retrograde. A lost love or abandoned hobby could suddenly assume new importance. You are highly imaginative and creative during the last week of July. Record ideas and thoughts that occur now for future reference. A visit to a formal garden or park near Lammastide could set the scene for a romance to blossom before your birthday. The hot, sensual days of early August find Venus continuing to bring delight as it transits your sign. It's time to relax, socialize, and purchase some new trinkets. Favorable transits in your 2nd house as the month ends brighten the financial picture, so you can afford to indulge a bit.

The New Moon in Virgo on September 3 is close to an opposition with Uranus in Pisces. An eccentric but intriguing individual can change your plans. Be careful of the expectations you have of others during the two weeks following this lunation. Only offer help or advice if it is requested three times. At the autumn equinox a supportive Mars influence in your 9th house favors physical activity to honor the harvest season. Your energy level will be especially high. October's eclipses impact both of your money houses. You may find your values changing. Welcome the opportunity to try something new if a familiar source of income suddenly disappears and all will be well. On all Hallows Eve Mercury begins a long passage through your 4th house of home and heritage. Thoughts will center on home life and understanding relatives. Avoid a change of residence from November 15–December 4 though. Mercury will be retrograde and the move would prove unsatisfactory. On November 6 Venus enters your sister Earth sign of Capricorn, linking to your love and romance sector. From then until just before Yuletide your social prospects will be really promising. A relationship with someone a little older or younger could be very successful. Use fragrant herbs such as rosemary and lavender in love rituals. The Earth sign emphasis in this trend favors calling on the plant kingdom.

Mid-December finds Mars completing its retrograde. If there have been travel-related glitches and delays these should be cleared up as 2005 ends. January begins with Mercury joining the Sun in Capricorn. You'll want to offer support to loved ones. Dedication to a worthwhile mutual interest could enhance a love bond. You won't feel the chill of the deep winter days because there are so many positive projects and relationships brightening the hours now. Devote the Candlemas sabbat to health rituals because your 6th house will be accented strongly. Stress release and yogic breathing can be magically employed to build a cone of healing power. The last three weeks of February through the end of winter Pisces transits, including Mercury, will oppose you. Listen to others' viewpoints. Compromise and negotiate. A lunar eclipse on March 14 in your sign promises surprises as winter ends. Be receptive to the unexpected near that date. You might even find that a whole new life is about to begin.

HEALTH

With Aquarius as ruler of your house of health, you are very receptive to alternative health care. A visit to a spa featuring massage, aromatherapy, healthy foods, and relaxing music for stress release would be worth considering. You are very prone to seasonal affective disorder and other weather-related conditions. Also, unusual and unexpected factors can impact your well-being. Your health condition can change very rapidly. Try not to make sudden decisions about treatments. Reflect a bit before leaping in.

LOVE

From late July until mid-February Mars, planet of desire and passion, is winking at you. Mars will spend all of that time in Taurus, favorably aspected to your Sun. This promises more enthusiasm about love in general for the often reserved and chaste Virgo. A really exciting and life-changing intimate relationship is possible. Since your 9th house is involved the attraction could involve someone who is very involved in higher education or who comes from another cultural background. The blossom of a friendship made while traveling could bloom into a true love rose.

SPIRITUALITY

Parables and storytelling sessions with a spiritual message can awaken you to the deeper aspects of mystical truths. Guidance comes while you examine an old book of fairy tales, reading between the lines, of course. Listen carefully to the lyrics of traditional ballads. The Full Moon of November 15 and the Virgo lunar eclipse on March 14 usher in cycles of spiritual experiences. Draw down the Moon on those evenings to intensify the process.

FINANCE

Three of the eclipses this year will highlight your 2nd and 8th houses, both of which are tied to finances and investments. The old rules are changing. New feelings and needs are arising. Stay well informed about any changes in your source of income or the demand for salable job skills. Adapting to meet new needs will enhance your security. With generous Jupiter in Libra, your 2nd house of cash flow, from the vernal equinox until late October you should be able to generate a comfortable income.

LIBRA

The year ahead for those
born under the sign of the Scales
September 24–October 23

Romantic yet rather flirtatious, you are a refined diplomat who must overcome the temptation to vacillate. Ruled by gracious Venus and the element air, your natural instincts lean toward restoring harmony and balance. Libra is the sign of marriage and partnership. Relationships of all kinds give true meaning to your life. In Babylon, the Scales belonged to Shamash, judge of heaven and Earth. He fathered two gods Kittu (justice) and Misharu (law). These divine offspring were called upon during divination sessions to assure a balanced and fair decision.

The vernal equinox finds Saturn poised, completing its retrograde, at the midheaven of your chart. Tremendous ambition and pressure to succeed in your career are building. Lucky Jupiter is in your sign and promises rewards, but you have demands to meet first. Venus will enter Aries, your opposing sign, during the week before All Fools' Day. Expect conflict between the needs of the heart and a desire to achieve. Shy away from any romantic involvements that lack sincerity. The April 8 eclipse impacts your relationships and may bring a shift regarding loyalties and commitments. Mercury will be in Aries through mid-May, in retrograde motion for much of that time. Make a special effort to communicate clearly and listen carefully.

On May 10 Venus will enter Gemini to create a grand trine in air signs with Neptune in Aquarius and Jupiter in Libra. This marks the start of one of the most fortunate cycles all year. Through Midsummer Eve both finances and relationships will be a delight. Honor the element air by hanging bells and wind chimes where they can be tickled by wayward breezes. During the last week of June Mars in Aries will aspect other cardinal sign transits, a pattern which sets a hectic pace until Lammastide. Associates are competitive throughout July, and some legal or ethical issues may come to the fore. Leo transits in your 11th house of friendship are well aspected, though. A true pal comes to your rescue and helps resolve a potentially sticky situation near July 18.

The retrograde Mercury period in early August is a good time for visits and saying thank you. On August 17 Venus glides into your sign where it is greeted by Jupiter. These benevolent planets conjoining your Sun will mark another stellar period of overall success. It will last until shortly before Mabon. Express creative ideas, attend cultural events, nurture relationships. Whatever you focus on will grow, so take care of what means the most to you.

The autumnal equinox finds Mercury entering your sign for a brief but favorable passage. Through October 8 travel will be enjoyable and successful. Your judgment is especially good, so don't go through the usual agony about making a decision. Your instincts will lead you to the right choices. The eclipses of October 3 and 17 profoundly impact Librans, especially those born during that two-week period. A new home, job, or relationship can replace the familiar. Don't resist changes; after an unsettled time all will be well. "It's time to grow," is the final message from Jupiter as it exits your sign on October 25, completing a year-long transit. Celebrate Samhain with peaceful rites recognizing death and rebirth metaphors. The Old Celtic New Year definitely feels like a fresh start.

November brings an emphasis on finances with Scorpio transits in your 2nd house. Hunt for bargains; be patient with negotiations. Check the credit history of those you do business with. Someone might not be trustworthy or skilled in money matters. The Taurus Full Moon of November 15 reveals the details. Late November through December 4 Mercury is retrograde in your 2nd and 3rd houses. Call ahead before running errands to avoid the proverbial wild goose chase. A last minute change of plans at Thanksgiving will turn out happily. Complete Yuletide preparations by December 15 for Venus will brighten your home and family sector then. After the winter solstice, Venus turns retrograde until February 4. Your vitality may be up and down. A little extra rest and a warm fire to chase away winter chills and doldrums are essential. Be good to yourself. Since your love and romance sector is impacted, a relationship can be in a sluggish or uncertain phase. Make no demands; be a true friend to the one you care for. Devote the Candlemas sabbat to brewing sweet and tender love magic. Prepare a gift of charmed chocolates to give on Valentine's Day.

Throughout the rest of winter Pisces transits accent your 6th house. Animals respond well to your love and care. Scatter seed for wild birds. A familiar provides comfort and companionship near the Pisces New Moon on February 27. When Venus enters Aquarius on March 6 a promising time begins regarding love and leisure time pursuits. Your artistic ability is excellent during the last days of winter. Try drawing, dancing, or photography.

HEALTH
The eclipses this year can propel you into new surroundings. Be alert to routine safety concerns. Create a comfortable environment. Some time and energy can be dedicated to the health needs of a loved one. When this occurs, remember to take to rest and regroup. Traditional Chinese medicines will offer you much, as your birth sign has a special link to the Orient. Acupuncture can work wonders for many Librans.

LOVE
The early spring finds Mars in Aquarius stirring fire into your romantic sector.

A magnetic attraction can develop in the weeks leading up to Beltane. The eclipses show so many changes around you, though, that a relationship might not stabilize until after the Venus retrograde is over in mid-February. May and mid-August through mid-September are times when Venus is well aspected, promising some dalliances and liaisons. Try the pink bubble technique. This is a simple yet potent visualization. Employ it by imagining a pink light expanding from your heart to engulf the one you care for. Create and project the pink bubble of light daily for four weeks starting on a New Moon.

SPIRITUALITY
Mercury, the planet of writers, has a link to the spiritual factors in your birth chart. Purchase a journal to record dreams and tidbits of mystical information. As you reread old entries you will be amazed at how much you've grown. Automatic writing and mastering the ouija board can help you connect with messages from spirit guides. This year the Midsummer sabbat is an especially good time to seek spiritual understanding. So is the month of October. Current publications about spiritual matters and the craft can be a source of valuable information. Attend discussion groups or book clubs which are dedicated to spiritual topics.

FINANCE
Your income should be increasing this year, due to the prominent Jupiter transit. At the same time your overhead can be high. There are challenging influences from Saturn and the eclipses. Wise money management and seeking good prices on costly items is the key to greater security. Sensitive Scorpio rules your finances. This is a reminder that your emotional state can impact monetary decisions. Postpone making financial decisions if you're upset. You could be too impulsive or too influenced by a loved one. This is not the time to take chances. Check your bank balance from time to time. Keep receipts so that you are able to obtain refunds in case of buyer's remorse.

SCORPIO

*The year ahead for those
born under the sign of the Scorpion*
October 24–November 22

Subtle and discerning, Scorpio is linked to rebirth, eternal life, and death. Pluto, planet of deep space and the unfathomable, rules this water sign. To achieve happiness, Scorpios must first resolve extremes of emotion. They recognize the power wielded by silence and secrecy. This creates a innate talent for all kinds of magical work. In spiritual manuscripts from the 12th century the Scorpion appears as a serpent which can cleverly disguise itself with a pleasant countenance. Selket of ancient Egypt was a Scorpion goddess who governed intimacy, passions, bliss, and ecstasy.

Spring begins with a strong accent on your health. Dedicate a vernal equinox ritual to healing and vitality. On March 27 Pluto turns retrograde in Sagittarius. Income is impacted by work you've done in the past and your established financial habits. An employment opportunity suggested by an old friend can be worth considering. Mars zips through your 4th house before May Eve. April is a wonderful time to cast out clutter and do a thorough spring cleaning. On April 24 a lunar eclipse in your sign promises some excitement and surprises. Welcome changes regarding work and creative projects.

Beltane is the time for love rituals. Mars will transit your 5th house of pleasure and romance from May 1–June 11. Someone you admire would enjoy going to a sporting event or taking an exercise class. The weeks leading up to Midsummer Day favor travel. Both Venus and Mercury will brighten your 9th house. June is also an excellent time to enroll in workshops and classes. Expand and explore. During July expect an energy shift; first Mercury and Venus, then the Sun and Saturn will enter Leo. This accents career and ambition. You'll be considered an authority and role model. This is satisfying, but also promises added responsibility. Your success will be affected by the effort you expend just before Lammastide. Double check contracts and communications related to your work while Mercury is retrograde July 23–August 16. Friends and partners will make plans for you and offer advice. Over the summer Mars begins a long passage through Taurus, your relationship sector. During the first half of August others will be especially concerned and helpful because Venus will be in Virgo, in a favorable aspect to Mars. This highlights the 11th house of wish fulfillment. You will be honored and appreciated.

Early September finds you relishing peace and quiet, for benevolent Venus and Jupiter will both be in your 12th house. Imagery and affirmations can bring contentment. On September 12 Venus enters Scorpio, a promising trend which lasts through October 7. Reach out to others; love and friendship are there if you're receptive. It's also a great time for creative projects. The October 17 eclipse has a message about your health. Take time to rest and nourish your body. Listen to its needs. Make any necessary changes related to wellness and all will be fine. The three weeks before Halloween find Mercury racing quickly and cleverly through your sign. Rapid responses are the path to success. Writing, travel, and learning are all favored.

There is much to celebrate at Samhain. Lucky Jupiter begins a year-long passage through your sign on October 26. A time of growth and opportunity commences. The Scorpio New Moon on November 1 brings a vision of the year to come. Select goals. This lunation has many fixed signs present. Commitments made will stick, so be cautious if considering a promise that could entangle. During November the Capricorn and Taurus transits of Venus and Mars, respectively, bring the financial needs and plans of others to the fore. Someone who seems selfish might just fear scarcity. Suggest employing prosperity consciousness. You'll earn their love and respect. From November 27–December 11 Mercury pauses in the last degrees of Scorpio, combining with a sextile aspect from Venus. It's a wonderful time for research, completing old business, and correspondence.

As the days grow shorter and Yule approaches, Mercury and the Sun move toward Pluto in your 2nd house. Check provisions and supplies; restock shelves and larders. Use that bit of extra cash you've been hoarding to make a purchase that will give you pleasure. January opens with an active 3rd house. Keep a sense of humor if a neighbor is difficult or eccentric. Remember, the world would be dull if we were all the same. Transportation arrangements will have to be revamped; say an incantation to the gods of roadways, call upon a friendly gypsy and you will be on your way again by the time of the Full Moon in Cancer on January 14. This lunation generates a sense of freedom and well-being. As Candlemas nears, planets will gather in your home and family sector. Examine ways to make housing as comfy and hospitable as possible. Neptune is involved with other Aquarius transits in this pattern, so dreams and hunches about domestic matters should be heeded.

On February 9 Mercury will join Uranus in the 5th house. Together they will see the winter through. Recreational activities that inspire thinking and learning will bring you happiness. Perhaps you might join a book club to find a new love. Encourage a potential love interest to talk. Listen. Children will be a source of comfort and joy. During meditation sessions in March a solution to a problem or a comforting message from the afterlife arrives.

HEALTH

The eclipses this year will affect your Sun, the life force and vitality, as well as your 12th and 6th houses. Be well informed about health. Honoring your body with rest and care will assure continued well-being. There can be some changes in fitness programs or your personal care regime to address. Don't exceed the limits of your endurance and all will be well.

LOVE

Near your birthday Jupiter's passage into Scorpio will have a positive impact on your appearance and personality. This powerful pattern will trine Uranus in Pisces which has been in the midst of a seven-year movement through your love and romance sector. The wonderful combination of these two water sign planets points to a memorable year for love. Set the scene by decorating your bedroom with a fountain and playing recordings of the waves and sea birds. Arrange for a moonlit walk along the shore with one you're drawn to. Let the magic take hold.

SPIRITUALITY

The Moon has a special tie to spirituality in your life. It rules your 9th house. Regularly observe esbats at the Full and New Moons with incantations and ritual. Delve into the deeper myths surrounding one of the many Moon goddesses and call upon her as a special patron. Diana, Hecate, Kaltes, Selene, Circe, and Kuan Yin are all wonderful choices.

FINANCE

Jupiter rules your 2nd house of finances. When it enters Scorpio in the autumn, a really prosperous cycle begins. The rewards of past labor will be realized. A Pluto trend has been adding a depth and intensity to security issues for many years. You have not wanted to labor merely for the money, but also for fulfillment on other levels. Offer thanks for all that you have. Expressing an attitude of gratitude will be the catalyst for even greater success in the future.

SAGITTARIUS

*The year ahead for those
born under the sign of the Archer*
November 23–December 21

Your independent spirit makes experience your best and only real teacher. The Centaur, the man-animal, is your emblem. On one level this symbol reveals how close Sagittarians are to animal companions. There is another message, though. The human torso atop the animal body shows how the higher nature can rise above the animal instincts to attain higher consciousness. The arrow speeding toward a target beautifully illustrates the energy of this final fire sign of winter. Brilliant and ephemeral, the fiery arrow calls to mind the transient beauty of the Aurora Borealis, the northern lights. Chiron, the kindly Centaur, was a beloved teacher and respected healer. He understood and guided young, wayward Centaurs.

At the vernal equinox, Mercury, the Sun, and Venus all smile — in your 5th house of love. By All Fools' Day you're delighting in the company of one you care for. The Aries eclipse of April 8 marks a turning point. Either an attraction ends abruptly or becomes a more significant part of your life. From April 14 through May Eve plan to commute. A Mars influence in your 3rd house shows numerous short, enjoyable journeys. You have a touch of spring fever and won't be able to keep still for long. From May 1-15 Mars moves into a conjunction with Uranus in the sector of home and family life. Relatives are unpredictable, and the home requires maintenance. Do a blessing to protect your dwelling place.

As June begins Jupiter, your ruler, completes a long retrograde cycle and turns direct in your 11th house. A new sense of direction and purpose develops. Accept invitations from friends or plan a get-together. By the summer solstice you'll realize the blessings of friendship. At the end of June a grand trine in the fire signs forms. Leo planets aspect Mars in Aries and Pluto in Sagittarius, allowing you to accomplish much in record time. Independence Day finds you delighting in fireworks displays and a late-night barbecue. A retrograde Mercury pattern in this same sector of your chart commences on July 23, supporting a nostalgic mood. By Lammas Venus will be in your 10th house. Creative ideas can help your career. An admirer gives you a positive recommendation as August begins. Mars is starting a long passage through your 6th house. Seek stress release. Animals may require extra time and expense. Consider carefully if adopting a new familiar or animal companion.

During the first week of September the New Moon in Virgo aspects Uranus, creating vacillation. Your heart tells you to focus on home and family life, but another part of you wants to advance at work. Make time for both. Balance is the key to success now. The autumn equinox brings a chance to step back and prioritize. Libra transits, including the Sun, form sextiles from your 11th house. October's eclipses are very significant regarding closest relationships and future plans. On October 8 Venus enters your sign, staying until November 5. Halloween will be very memorable. If you host a Samhain event it will be a spectacular success. Your popularity and charm are in top form. November 1 finds Mercury moving into your sign where it favorably aspects Saturn by midmonth. Intellectual curiosity is heightened. It's a good time to enroll in classes or visit a book club.

Jupiter is beginning a year-long passage through Scorpio where it will probe the depths of your mysterious 12th house. Suddenly discretion is more important than usual. You'll cherish your privacy.

Quiet, good deeds generate positive karma. You'll be aware of the secret worries and needs of others. There are opportunities now to be helpful, almost acting like a sort of guardian angel to those less fortunate. December 1 finds the Sagittarius New Moon in your 1st house. It's easy to express yourself over the next two weeks. Focus on image improvement. Celebrate your birthday with some new wardrobe items. From December 13 through New Year's Eve 2006 Mercury will move rapidly through your sign, conjoining the Sun and Pluto as it goes. You'll be able to accurately assess situations. Travel over the Yuletide holiday season would be very successful.

Venus in Capricorn retrogrades through your money sector from early January until February 4. It's time to conserve on expenses. There may be temporary tension with a loved one about finances. Remember what's really important and be patient when working with expenses. Don't indulge in hurtful words toward a loved one if money management becomes frustrating. During the last three weeks of February relatives show new talents and versatility. Mercury joins Uranus in your home and family sector. Interesting events, conversations, and visitors make the domestic environment more lively. On February 18 Mars enters Gemini, your opposing sign. Competitive feelings may be present. Partners exhibit a take-charge attitude. Cooperate. Teamwork is the key to success now. After March 6 Venus in Aquarius brightens your communication sector. Your clever use of words will make an impression. Promote ideas and make suggestions as winter ends.

HEALTH
Lemon balm is a healing herb that has a traditional association with your birth sign. Brew tea from the fragrant leaves as you meditate on the legendary Lord Llewellyn of Wales. He credited his long and healthy 110-year life span to a daily drink of lemon balm tea. Your health sector is ruled by Taurus. Mars remains in that sign from late July until February. Control anger and impatience to minimize accident hazards during this time. Don't overdo hard physical work or stay too long in the Sun. Gradual exposure and avoiding extremes are your keys to wellness now.

LOVE
Eclipses in Aries, your 5th house of romance, promise sparkles and surprises in matters of the heart this year. Near April 8 and October 17 significant meetings and partings can occur. You always enjoy a challenge in love situations and can lose interest in someone who is too complacent. March 23–April 15, June 29–July 22 and October 8–November 4 mark positive Venus influences. Love connections are likely to strike the right chord combining excitement with harmony to equal happiness at those times.

SPIRITUALITY
In July Saturn begins a long passage through Leo, your 9th house of higher thought. This combination indicates a special link to the long-ago and faraway. Regressive hypnosis, including past life study, can be an effective aid in spiritual awareness. Also, antiques and scrapbooks may have messages. A recollection by a grandparent shared with a grandchild can play a part in spiritual awakening, especially during July and August.

FINANCE
Capricorn and Cancer rule your money houses. You often have luck at sales and discount stores. The impact others have on your personal finances has been considerable over the past year, due to a transit in Cancer. You'll have a greater sense of control after Lammas. Venus is in your money sector from January until early March. Dedicate the Candlemas sabbat to money magic. An effective ritual would be to take a bright green pillar candle, surround it with a circle of gold dollars, and then drizzle the coins with honey and cinnamon. Burn the candle, letting the melting wax cover everything. Clean the coins in rain water and carry them in a silken bag for luck.

CAPRICORN

*The year ahead for those
born under the sign of the Goat*
December 22–January 20

Step by step, the Goat perseveres. Ambitious, prudent, solemn, and reliable he respectfully greets the winter solstice atop the sacred mountain. This earth sign of deep winter has a special link with time. Always feeling that the best is yet to come, Saturn's children are serious, seeming most content when studying and working. Paradoxically there is a light-hearted, even jolly mood projected by older Capricorns. Ea, a Babylonian god whose name means "palace of waters" was a fish-tailed goat.

Spring's first days find Saturn, your ruler, turning direct in Cancer. Old business regarding partnership and legal matters is concluded. The vernal equinox brings a fresh start regarding relationships. By All Fools' Day there's a strong accent on your home and family sector. Devote the first half of April to making happy changes in living arrangements and helping family members reach goals. Hang an updated photo of your family in your work space to symbolize the positive interaction of home with professional life. Through Beltane Mars will be in your 2nd house of finance. You'll be working hard at security issues. Follow a hunch about a business matter near April 14 when Mars conjoins Neptune. Your insight proves lucrative. Show appreciation for the creations and accomplishments of a loved one during June. Venus in your 7th house brings success to a partner. Near Midsummer Day use care regarding business meetings and travel. A Mercury-Saturn conjunction in opposition to you hints at some delays or frustration.

On June 22 the first of two Full Moons in your sign promises a very active schedule. Versatility helps. During July Saturn joins other Leo transits in your 8th house. Messages from the spirit world should be heeded. The second Full Moon (a rarity) in Capricorn is on July 21. Do background research and check claims others make as it's close to an out-of-sign opposition involving Saturn. Near Lammas your feelings will be very intense. Add a note of humor if you sense you're coming across as overly opinionated. Be true to yourself, yet sensitive to the needs of companions. Observe others' facial expressions in order to maintain perspective. During August, Mars and Venus will be in your sister Earth signs of Taurus and Virgo, respectively. This ushers in a time of accomplishment. Financial and spiritual riches are multiplying in your life. Honor the earth elementals with drum music followed by an outdoor meditation.

During early September the Sun and Mercury are favorably placed in your 9th house. Imported foods or music have appeal. Incantations in another language add depth and power to your ritual work in preparation for the autumn equinox. The October 3 eclipse in Libra activates Jupiter in your 10th house of career and recognition. New horizons beckon; a phase of your professional life is ending. Be receptive to changes. Hints about the specifics are in the air by Samhain. During early November, Venus begins a long transit through Capricorn. Commit early to plans and invitations for Thanksgiving and Yule. Holiday events emphasizing art and music are especially worthwhile. Brighten autumn's darkening days by offering tokens to those whom you admire. If these are items you've made, so much the better.

On December 1 the New Moon in Sagittarius impacts a grouping of planets in your 12th house. Until Yule your dreams will be especially vivid. Take the time to interpret them and valuable messages will emerge. Untamed places and wild animals will recognize the innermost you. Don't worry if you're unable to share some of these feelings at present. The Capricorn New Moon on December 30 ushers in a cycle of greater external expression. On January 4 Mercury enters your sign where it favorably aspects the Sun, Venus, and Mars before Candlemas. This is perfect for multitasking with aplomb. Make decisions, plan studies, and travel. February 4 finds Venus turning direct in your sign, accompanied by a strong 2nd house influence. During the rest of the month your financial situation steadily brightens. Use the added abundance to do good for yourself and others. The February 13 Full Moon, on the eve of Valentine's Day, will show you the way.

During March planets in Gemini, Pisces, and Sagittarius activate houses in your birth chart. Plan for the future by establishing good habits. Conversations can be a little confusing. Insist upon clarity. During winter's final days Jupiter turns retrograde in your 11th house of wishes and friendships. People from the past call or visit. You'll feel haunted by an old wish or goal which proved elusive. Be very realistic if you're tempted to give it another try. Practical guidelines provide the best route to success just now.

HEALTH

With changeable Gemini ruling your 6th house of health you can be ambivalent about fitness. If you understand the logical reasons behind exercise programs, checkups, etc. you are more likely to follow through with them. Be well informed. The New Moon on June 6 aspects Jupiter, the celestial healer, beautifully. That lunation ushers in a four-week period during which you can effectively work on your health, making changes for the better. Saturn has been in opposition to your Sun, having a draining affect on the health of those close to you. That trend is over in July. When your concerns for others lessen, you should experience an enhanced vitality.

LOVE

Mars, planet of passion, remains a very long time in Taurus, your 5th house of romance this year. From July 29–February 17 your physical magnetism will be exceptionally high. A passionate yet sometimes stormy relationship is on the horizon. Venus, the love goddess, smiles sweetly at Mars during a very long transit in your sign. This spans most of the period from November 6–March 5. The heavenly lovers lingering in the Earth signs for so long are promising you a genuinely joyful year regarding matters of the heart. Plan a picnic, mountain hike, or camping trip to set the scene for a happy interlude

SPIRITUALITY

Mystical Neptune's current influence in your financial sector shows that spending money for spiritual growth would be worthwhile. Create a home meditation area decked out with new items dedicated to spiritual awakening. Just after All Hallows Venus begins to influence you strongly. Venus rules beautiful colors. During the late autumn and winter, try color healing to awaken higher consciousness. Learn more about the chakras. Try scheduling an aura photograph or chakra balancing with a reputable practitioner of parapsychology. It should be very rewarding. Meditate on the rainbow; look into its history and deeper spiritual symbolism.

FINANCE

There has been quite a bit of financial stress, mostly connected to high overhead or old debts, this past year. Jupiter and Saturn in square aspect in cardinal signs in your angular houses created it. That's about to change. In July Saturn enters Leo, your 8th house, where it remains throughout the end of the year. Fate takes a hand in the direction of your money situation. Investments, tax returns, insurance settlements, or possibly an inheritance are involved. At the end of October Jupiter enters Scorpio, creating a hopeful and nourishing influence. Friends can offer financial opportunities. The path to realizing a long cherished financial goal opens during the autumn and winter months. Enlist help from the gnomes. Make them an offering of gilded acorns at Yuletide.

AQUARIUS

The year ahead for those
born under the sign of the Water Bearer
January 21–February 19

Unpredictable and independent, you are a humanitarian reformer with a contrary streak. Airy and intellectual, fixed in your ways and opinions, your desire to befriend others is illustrated by your emblem, The Water Bearer. The human figure, usually male, generously pours a double stream of water to all. Ruled by Uranus, planet of science, enlightenment, and the New Age, Aquarius is a heroic figure offering hope following the darkest of nights. The Algonquin tribe of the Native Americans portrayed her as Nokomis, Mother Earth, blessing the ground with sacred water.

Enthusiasm and motivation are keynotes as spring begins. Mars enters your sign to remain until May Eve. Direct effort into problem solving if anger starts to erupt. The Mars energy, like fire, must be handled with care if it is to do good. As Mars nears Neptune during the week of April 14 your creative potential is very promising. Express it. The eclipse of April 24 highlights your 10th house. Prepare for change regarding professional aspirations. Be observant. If you have truly wanted a new career path, this is the time to pursue it.

Early June finds Venus, the Sun, and Mercury in Gemini making a promising aspect pattern in your love and pleasure sector. On June 6 Jupiter turns direct in Libra, activating a wonderful grand trine. Friends and lovers may change roles. Travel opportunities are very promising through the summer solstice. Don't let potentials slip away. Do your part to let a memorable experience unfold. With the strong air sign presence in June, learn all you can about the magical qualities of wind as well as sacred breath work.

As July begins, wellness is important. Both the Sun and Saturn accent your health sector. Reach fitness goals with patience and attention to detail. The impact of longtime health habits becomes apparent by the Full Moon on July 21. That's an excellent time to draw down the lunar energy for healing. Water therapies can be especially effective. By Lammas Saturn will have joined retrograde Mercury in Leo, your 7th house of relationships. In early August choices must be made regarding loyalty and commitment. Others cling to you, a situation which can be uncomfortable for the free-spirited Uranian. The Full Moon in your sign on August 19 illuminates the options and can mark a turning point. Since this lunation is closely aspected to Neptune, a dream or psychic vision should be heeded. Your intuition is on target. The end of August through September 10 finds a happy Venus in Libra transit in your 9th house. Travel, try creative writing. Someone from another cultural or spiritual background can become a romantic prospect or at least a new friend.

At the autumn equinox several fixed sign transits, including Mars in Taurus and Saturn in Leo, find you faced with some rigidity. Play by the rules patiently; make the most of the status quo. Short cuts won't work right now. Hesitate if you're contemplating a residential move. On October 2 Mars turns retrograde, lessening stress and giving you a reprieve. The lunar eclipse in Aries on October 17 activates your 3rd house. Ideas suggested in casual conversation are worth examining. Read current magazines and newspapers. You're about to learn something valuable quite by accident. Impromptu journeys add dimension to your life in the weeks before All Hallows.

November finds Mercury in Sagittarius backing into a retrograde spiral in your 11th house. Pluto watches from the sidelines. Longtime acquaintances will be in touch. You'll be quite surprised by the changes in their lives. On November 16 Uranus turns direct in your financial sector. Money matters brighten during the weeks before Yule. Expect a favorable turn of events regarding a new business or employment opportunity. From December 15 through New Year's Day 2006 Venus will be hovering at the brink of your sign. A flurry of interesting invitations can come along. You will greatly enjoy seasonal treats and music at that time. Devote the winter solstice sabbat to love magic.

During the first three weeks of January a stellium of Capricorn planets in your 12th house points to a need for some extra rest and retreat. Energy will be replenished and you'll be able to get organized during hours of peaceful solitude. By January 29, the day of the New Moon in Aquarius, you will be ready to be more interactive. That lunation activates Mercury and Neptune's influences, also in your sign. By Candlemas your writing and speaking abilities win you admiration and love. Your personality and appearance create a memorable impression on influential individuals. Take the lead in making suggestions and arranging projects near your birthday. After February 19 the Sun joins Uranus and Mercury in Pisces to emphasize your 2nd house of income and security. You feel the need to acquire more security and also to shop for some desired items. On March 6 Venus enters Aquarius, adding a happy energy to the rest of the month. Matters of the heart and financial prospects are extremely promising during the end days of winter.

HEALTH
The changeable and inconsistent Moon holds sway over your 6th house of health. Your health condition is prone to sudden changes. Recovery as well as relapses can occur instantaneously, in fact. Keep a health diary for a few months, recording how you feel as each moon sign and phase passes. This will create a valuable tool for being in tune with your own health rhythms. Mushrooms are ruled by the Moon and have been credited with healing power since ancient times. Collect a variety of mushroom recipes to try.

LOVE
A Beltane flirtation blooms into a more intimate romance by the summer solstice. Venus cheers the situation on from your 5th house of love and pleasure. Jupiter in Libra, sign of marriage, supports the pattern with an encouraging trine aspect. In July Saturn begins a passage of more than two years through Leo, which rules your relationships. Responsibility, commitment, and a reality check directly linked to marriage issues are a certainty. A partner might need more encouragement and support from you. Patience is important, but be honest and let go if a situation just isn't working. An age difference can be a factor to consider regarding one you cherish.

SPIRITUALITY
On October 3 a solar eclipse in Libra awakens great spiritual potential. It falls in your 9th house and trines mystical Neptune in your sign. Invest in some metaphysical reference books. Tarot and numerology are excellent topics to delve into during the weeks before Samhain. Collect crystals and unusual beads. Design your own talismans and charm bags. This year you are especially responsive to the spiritual energies in jewelry. An antique ring or pendant found quite by chance can carry a marvelous mystical aura.

FINANCE
Uranus, your ruler, is retrograde in your 2nd house of finances from June 15–November 16. Timing can be a factor in money management. Be aware of when payments are due and when income can be expected to arrive. From Thanksgiving on, your originality generates more income. A Uranus-Jupiter pattern in water signs before Yule makes others appreciate your efforts and tend to reward you financially. Apply for positions which have promise and potential this year. Muster the confidence to try to boost your earnings. You can do it.

PISCES

*The year ahead for those
born under the sign of the Fish*
February 20–March 20

Subtle, receptive, and compassionate yet veiled with a vague otherworldliness, Pisces can be the most complex of the zodiac's signs. The Fish swim in opposite directions while seeking a purposeful goal. Yearning to be loved and accepted, Pisceans often see and hear circumstances the way they would like them to be. In Syria Pisces links to the goddess Atargatis, who descended into a pool and emerged with fins and a tail. Ascending back to heaven, Atargatis was accompanied by two fishes. They were lost to Earth when they became the constellation Pisces.

As spring begins observe all omens with the number seven linked to them. This is the number of Uranus. Uranus, the cosmic transformer, is in the midst of a seven-year passage through Pisces. Seven signifies exclusiveness and spirituality as well as ancient wisdom. The sevens will bring a valuable hint of what the year to come means by All Fools' Day. During April your 2nd house is strong. Mercury, Venus, the Sun as well as the solar eclipse early in the month all accent it. Conversations will revolve around business and earning powers. A hobby or creative talent can have income producing potential. At Beltane Mars enters Pisces, giving you energy and enthusiasm through June 11. Much can be accomplished during this period, but do keep anger in check.

As the summer solstice nears Venus, Mercury, and Saturn in Cancer all cluster in your love sector. The prominent water signs in this sky picture bring a sensitive and sentimental mood to love. Photos, scrapbook souvenirs, and walks along the shore will delight someone you care for. Devote the summer solstice sabbat to love magic. The end of June brings some turbulence from Mars in your 2nd house of finances. Through July 28 control any anger or impatience related to financial situations. Impulsive purchases or hasty financial decisions are not favored. As Lammas draws near Mercury goes retrograde in your 6th house. Good health habits are a must. Honor your body and serve healthy foods at the August 1 sabbat festivities. An animal that strays to your door may belong to someone else. Don't consider it a permanent part of your household until after August 16 when Mercury retrograde concludes. During the rest of August Venus moves rapidly through Libra, your 8th house, in a quincunx aspect involving your Pisces Sun. There's a sense of fate in the air. Adapt to circumstances. Keep perspective if love and emotional issues grow complex. September brings valuable insights from close associates, for Mercury races with the Sun through Virgo, your opposing sign. The September 3 New Moon in Virgo can bring an important new partnership. Creativity is enhanced by the Full Moon in your sign on September 17. That lunation aspects Venus favorably and conjoins Uranus.

October's eclipse pattern highlights security and values. Your perception of what true wealth really is will be examined. Inherited or invested funds can be involved in financial planning. Adapt to changes at a place of employment or in the world economic condition as a whole. On October 26 Jupiter begins a year-long passage through Scorpio, promising a significant change for the better. You'll be able to appreciate all that you have. Spiritual practices such as affirmation and visualization will manifest in real wealth. A breakthrough can be expected for Pisceans who have been working to perfect a skill or complete a program of higher education. During November and early December your 10th house is highlighted by

Mercury, Pluto, and eventually the Sun. A presentation before a group could inspire the confidence of business associates. Do research connected to career goals. The additional information can open a real window of opportunity by Yuletide.

2006 begins with Capricorn planets sextile your Sun. Organize goals. Make lists to guide you through the days to come. A sense of camaraderie builds and you're truly thankful for your friends. From January 23–February 8 your 12th house is especially active with Mercury touching the Sun and your ruler, Neptune, there. Burn white candles during the evenings to placate the spirits of ice and snow. Honor solitude in observing Candlemas. The stillness of deep winter is healing. Guidance comes from within following a dream or deep meditation. Just before Valentine's Day Mercury joins Uranus to transit in conjunction with your Sun. This sets the pace for the rest of the winter and rewards you with greater mental energy. It's also easier to solve problems and make wise choices. Travel is interesting and rewarding now as well. On March 3 Mercury turns retrograde. This ushers in a wonderful time for visiting old haunts and childhood scenes. Contact a longtime acquaintance who has been out of touch. There is no mirror like an old friend. Gaze into the eyes of one of yours; you will be amazed to see how much you've grown.

HEALTH
Leo and the Sun rule your 6th house of health. Sunlight is a natural antiseptic. In moderation, try sunbathing to enhance vitality and strengthen the immune system. Saturn is entering Leo for about a two-year stay on July 17. Maintaining good health may take more time and effort from then on. Have a routine checkup near that time and practice good preventative measures. Make a special effort to plan a proper diet and regular exercise program. In the months ahead you will be rewarded.

LOVE
Since Cancer, the heavenly Moonchild, rules your love sector, the Moon's signs and phases offer clues about love prospects. Usually Full Moons will generate romantic connections, especially when they happen to fall in a water sign. The lunar eclipse at the Scorpio Full Moon on April 24 brings the hand of fate into play. The Pisces and Cancer lunations on September 17 and January 14, respectively will also be friendly to making a heart connection. Family gatherings and the matchmaking efforts of relatives can help set the scene for love as well.

SPIRITUALITY
Since an eclipse is affecting the spiritual sector of your chart near Beltane, there could be an attraction to new types of ritual and worship by late spring. This hints that you'll find a new meaning concerning what the practice of witchcraft really is to you. Just before All Hallows Eve Jupiter will enter your 9th house, Scorpio, for a year-long stay. This ushers in one of the most promising of all spiritual growth cycles. Consider focusing on deeper studies in metaphysics or comparative philosophy. Travel can also heighten spirituality.

FINANCE
Mercury begins the year in your money sector. It's a long Mercury transit, lasting through May 12. There could be multiple sources of income or your job duties can become more complicated in the early weeks of spring. If seeking employment, more than one opportunity arises. Two eclipses impact your financial sector, one on April 8, the other on October 17. Be alert to changes in your field as a whole. An old phase related to earnings and income could end, followed by a new beginning. The long transit of Mars through Taurus, from late July until mid-February activates your 3rd house favorably. This sector ties to practical education. Vocational education and on-the-job training is worth considering at that time.

THE FOX IN OLD JAPAN

An excerpt from *Glimpses of Unfamiliar Japan* (1894) by Lafcadio Hearn

BY EVERY SHADY WAYSIDE and in every ancient grove, on almost every hilltop and in the outskirts of every village, you may see, while traveling through the country, some little Shinto shrine, before which, or at either side of which, are images of seated foxes in stone. Usually there is a pair of these, facing each other. But there may be a dozen, or a score, or several hundred, in which case most of the images are very small.

In the neighborhood of the capital and in Tokyo itself, sometimes in the cemeteries, very beautiful idealized figures of foxes may be seen, elegant as greyhounds. They have long green or gray eyes of crystal quartz or some other diaphanous substance; and they create a strong impression as mythological conceptions.

But throughout the interior, fox images are much less artistically fashioned. The rustic foxes have no grace: they are uncouth; but they betray in countless queer ways the personal fancies of their makers. They are of many moods — whimsical, apathetic, inquisitive, saturnine, jocose, ironical; they watch and snooze and squint and wink and sneer; they wait with lurking smiles; they listen with cocked ears most stealthily.

There is an amusing individuality about them all, and an air of knowing mockery about most of them, even those whose noses have been broken off. Moreover, these country foxes have certain natural beauties which their modern Tokyo kindred cannot show. Time has bestowed upon them divers speckled coats of beautiful soft colors while they have been sitting on their pedestals, listening to the ebbing and flowing of the centuries and snickering weirdly at mankind. Their backs are clad with finest green velvet of old mosses; their limbs are spotted and their tails are tipped with the dead gold or dead silver of delicate fungi.

Inari, the name by which the Fox-God is generally known, signifies "Lord-of-Rice." Inari is not worshipped as the God of Rice only; indeed, there are many Inari, just as in antique Greece there are many deities called Hermes, Zeus, Athena, Poseidon — one in the knowledge of the learned, but essentially different in the imagination of the common people. Inari has been multiplied by reason of his different attributes.

Inari is often worshipped as a healer; and still more frequently as a deity having power to give wealth. (Perhaps because all the wealth of Old Japan was reckoned in *koku* of rice.) Therefore his foxes are sometimes represented holding keys in their mouths. I have never seen an image of Inari yet in any Inari temple.

Indeed, the old conception of the Deity of rice-fields has been overshadowed and almost effaced among the lowest classes by a weird cult totally foreign to the spirit of pure Shinto, the Fox-cult. The worship of the retainer has almost replaced the worship of the god. But in the course of centuries the Fox usurped divinity. And the stone images of him are not the only outward evidences of his cult. At the rear of almost every Inari temple you will generally find in the wall of the shrine building, on or two feet above the ground, an aperture about eight inches in diameter and perfectly circular. This circular orifice is a Fox-hole, and if you look within, you will probably see offerings of tofu or other food which foxes are supposed to be fond of. You will also, most likely, find grains of rice scattered on some little projection of woodwork below or near the hole, and you may see some peasant clap his hands before the hole, utter some little prayer, and swallow a grain or two of that rice in the belief that it will either cure or prevent sickness.

Now the fox for whom such a hole is made is an invisible fox, a phantom fox — the fox respectfully referred to by the peasant as *O-Kitsune-San*. If he ever suffers himself to become visible, his color is said to be snowy white.

T'a Ki, the cruel and beautiful concubine of the last emperor of the Shang dynasty, as depicted by Hokusai. Her scattered ashes were said to have turned into a many-tailed fox.

From the *Manga*, 1819

81

All foxes have supernatural power. There are good and bad foxes. The Inari fox is good, and the bad foxes are afraid of the Inari-fox. To define the fox-superstition at all is difficult, not only on account of the confusion of ideas on the subject among the believers themselves, but also on account of the variety of elements out of which it has been shapen. Its origin is Chinese but in Japan it became oddly blended with the worship of a Shinto deity, and again modified and expanded by the Buddhist concepts of thaumaturgy and magic. So far as the common people are concerned, it is perhaps safe to say that they pay devotion to foxes chiefly because they fear them. The peasant still worships what he fears.

Many declare that the fox never really assumes human shape; but that he only deceives people into the belief that he does so by a sort of magnetic power, or by spreading about them a certain magical effluvium. Innumerable are the stories told or written about the wiles of fox-women, but the fox does not always appear in the guise of a woman for evil purposes. The fox is never at a loss for a disguise; he can assume more forms than Proteus. Furthermore, he can make you see or hear or imagine whatever he wishes you to see, hear, or imagine.

It is believed that the Man-fox (*Hito-kitsune*) cannot be seen. But if he goes close to still water, his shadow can be seen in the water. Those "having foxes" are supposed to avoid the vicinity of rivers and ponds. The invisible fox, as already stated, attaches himself to persons. Like a Japanese servant, he belongs to the household.

But the cost of nourishing foxes is the least evil connected with the keeping of them. Foxes have no fixed code of ethics, and have proved themselves untrustworthy servants. They may initiate and long maintain the prosperity of some family; but should some grave misfortune fall upon that family in spite of the efforts of its invisible retainers, then these will suddenly flee away, taking all the valuables of the household along with them.

For all these reasons, and doubtless many more, people believed to have foxes are shunned. Inter-marriage with a fox-possessing family is out of the question; and many a beautiful and accomplished girl cannot secure a husband because of the popular belief that her family harbors foxes.

Now the belief in foxes does not affect persons only: it affects property. The land of a family supposed to have foxes cannot be sold at a fair price. People are afraid to buy it; for it is believed the foxes may ruin the new proprietor.

When a fox comes to your house at night and knocks, there is a peculiar muffled sound about the knocking by which you can tell that the visitor is a fox — if you have experienced ears. For a fox knocks at doors with its tail. If you open, then you will see a man, or perhaps a beautiful girl, who will talk to you only in fragments of words, but nevertheless in such a way that you can perfectly understand.

A man going home one night saw a fox running for its life pursued by dogs. He beat the dogs off with his umbrella, thus giving the fox a chance to escape. On the following evening he heard someone knock at his door, and on opening the door saw a very pretty girl standing there, who said to him: "Last night I would have died but for your august kindness. I know not how to thank you enough: this is only a pitiable little present." And she laid a small bundle at his feet and went away. He opened the bundle and found two beautiful ducks and two pieces of silver money — those long, heavy, leaf-shaped pieces of money — each worth ten or twelve dollars — such as are now eagerly sought for by collectors of antique things. After a little while, one of the coins changed before his eyes into a piece of glass; the other was always good.

Vast is the literature on the subject of foxes — ghostly foxes. Some of it is old as the 11th century. In the ancient romances and the modern cheap novel, in historical traditions and in popular fairytales, foxes perform wonderful parts. There are very beautiful and very sad and very terrible stories about foxes. There are legends of foxes discussed by great scholars, and legends of foxes known to every child in Japan.

But these strange beliefs are swiftly passing away. Year by year more shrines of Inari crumble down, never to be rebuilt. Year by year the statuaries make fewer images of foxes. Year by year fewer victims of fox-possession are taken to the hospitals to be treated according to the best scientific methods by Japanese physicians trained in Europe.

A Japanese family summons fox spirits with table tilting and music

83

Cupid and Psyche

"The Most Pleasant and Delectable Tale of Cupid and Psyche." An irresistible title, romping right into "Immortal Venus, born from the deep blue sea and risen to Heaven from its foam, has descended to earth and is now incarnate as a mortal at whom everyone is allowed to gaze." The mortal is Psyche, youngest of a king's three daughters. So begins what many consider the most exquisite of all classical myths, replete with dizzying levels of subtext.

Crowds sing praises to the princess, offer tributes, a cult arises. Venus finds her own altars bare. "I will give her cause to repent of so unlawful a beauty," the Goddess of Beauty vows. "No man will ever offer her marriage." She enlists the aid of her adored son, Cupid, the God of Love. "Infuse into the bosom of that haughty girl a passion for some low, mean being," she commands. The obedient son does so, but is so startled by her beauty that he accidently wounds himself with an arrow and Love falls in love.

The king is mystified that his legendary daughter inspires much homage but fails to awaken love. He consults an oracle, who divulges that Psyche "is destined to be bride of no mortal lover." Her husband will be a monster, and the princess must be abandoned on a cliff to meet her fate.

The royal parents are consumed with grief, but the oracle's word is divine edict. Psyche is conveyed to the mountain, where she discovers a magnificent palace. The princess enters timidly and is dazzled by marble floors, golden pillars, and all conceivable treasures. She sees no one, but everything is hers to enjoy. Invisible hands lead Psyche to an aromatic bath and clothe her in silks that ripple softly like brook water. Lovely music fills the air: singing, flutes, lutes. A table offers delicate foods and wines. Then invisible hands lead her to a bed of softest down.

The terrified maiden awaits her destined bridegroom. It is Cupid, invisible. His voice is soft with love and rich with passion. Soon Psyche returns his caresses. He comes only with darkness and flees before the first rays of the sun. The adoring bride begs her beloved to reveal himself, but he refuses. "If you saw me, perhaps you would fear me, perhaps adore me, but all I ask of you is to love me."

In time Psyche begs to let her sisters visit. Cupid gives his unwilling consent, and her sisters arrive. They are jealous of Psyche's magnificence and inflate her curiosity and fear. "Bring a lamp and peek at him when he is asleep," they advise. "And bring a sharp knife. If he is a monster, cut off his head."

Their words have poisoned Psyche's mind. When her bridegroom is asleep, she brings her oil lamp and a knife to the bridal bed. She sees the most beautiful of gods, known to the Greeks as Eros, "with golden curls and ringlets wandering over his snowy neck and crimson cheek, with two dewy wings on his shoulders, whiter than snow, and with shining feathers like the tender blossoms of spring." And as Psyche bends over him, a drop of burning oil falls on his shoulder and wounds him. "Is this how you repay my love? Love cannot dwell with suspicion," he says.

The castle disappears and grief-stricken Psyche, who is with child, wanders day and night in search of her beloved. Finally she is received by the angry Venus, who is caring for her wounded son. The goddess declares that Psyche is "ill-favored and disagreeable," and can only merit her divine husband if she performs three tasks. Venus sets Psyche monumental labors, which she performs thanks to Cupid's invisible aid. And since he has recovered from his wound, Cupid pleads his case with Jupiter, who persuades Venus to allow the lovesick couple to marry.

Psyche is wafted to the heavenly assembly, where Jupiter offers her a cup of ambrosia. "Drink this, Psyche, and be immortal; nor shall Cupid ever break away from the knot in which he is tied, but these nuptials shall be perpetual." The gods attend a great wedding breakfast. And in due time the couple have a daughter whose name is Voluptas, or Pleasure.

The source of the story is *Metamorphoses*, also known as *The Golden Ass*, the only complete Latin novel that has survived the era. Its author, Lucius

Psyche   Edward Burne-Jones, 1869

Apuleius, is a 2nd-century writer from a Roman colony in what is now Algeria. The book is sexy and raucous, the forerunner of Boccaccio and Rabelais, and tells the tale of a fool who dabbles in magic and turns himself into an ass. The Cupid and Psyche myth, derived from the Greek, is a nugget embedded in the basic gold mine of the plot.

Like all myths it is allegorical. Psyche is the Greek word for both "soul" and "butterfly." The butterfly reflects an enchanting image. It is symbolic of the soul released as the beautiful wings take flight from the groveling caterpillar and flutter into the heavens. In such a way Psyche, as the vital principle of Soul, is reconciled to the divine by the power of Love. But Cupid and Psyche are also down to earth. The couple represents mundane love as perfection — the union of passion and soul.

— BARBARA STACY

Seal of the Magi

Protecting the privacy and assuring the authenticity of personal messages has been an important concern since time immemorial. Just as no person of integrity would open another's letter or e-mail today, no one would tamper with a wax seal in bygone times. The breaking of a seal, except by the intended recipient, implies treachery and a broken trust. Love letters and betrothals as well as official documents and decrees were once protected by individual seals. In medieval Europe nearly every literate individual had one or several personal seals. Few of these have survived, for tradition decreed that a seal be destroyed on the death of the owner.

For over two thousand years special wax has been used to affix the seal's imprint to correspondence. Some of the earliest examples come from China during the Shang dynasty, found in archaeological sites at Anyang. A legend tells us that the first seal was given to the Emperor and brought by a dragon. Another version recounts a boat trip by Emperor Yao during which he receives a seal. The common thread is that a heavenly and divine quality exists about seals. Possessing one implies a mandate and elevated authority. Affixing a wax seal is a statement that a document is written by one's own hand. Seals have also been used to attest to the genuineness of calligraphy and other works of art.

One of the first projects undertaken by Thomas Jefferson, Benjamin Franklin and John Adams after signing the Declaration of Independence was to create a Great Seal for the United States. The magic of sealing wax and seals prevails, surviving amid the sophisticated methods of communication in today's high tech cyber space environment. Probably sealing wax will still be with us in another two thousand years, outlasting or holding its own alongside the fax machine and computer terminal. The personal flair as well as the dignity and prestige conferred by a wax seal is treasured by heads of state as well as people of all ages and circumstances, particularly practitioners of magic and artists. At the writing desk of the witch, craft projects and greeting cards as well as crucial messages concerning coven matters all lend themselves to being presented with a distinctive special seal of approval.

A signet ring, collectible coin, soapstone or hardwood carving attached to a base can all be used to imprint sealing wax. An array of commercially made seals can be purchased as well. Angels, owls, butterflies, zodiac signs, hearts and flowers are among the choices available. Experiment to find the one that best reflects your own style and philosophy. Using wax seals contributes greatly to the impact of correspondence. Remember, the unusual always attracts.

Once set, a seal should not be removable except by destroying it. Seals are meant to be broken upon receipt, of course. Sometimes a ribbon is inserted into the wax before imprinting to further protect an important missive against intrusion or worse — the seal being surreptitiously removed and placed on another document.

Sealing wax differs from candle wax, for sealing wax must have a distinctive texture and be much thicker. A good sealing wax is created by mixing a variety of ingredients. Since the 16th century, when it was imported from India, shellac has been used. Rosins from coniferous trees, beeswax and turpentine combined with a variety of pigments will yield waxes that are attractive and secure. Prussian blue, vermilion, verdigris, fine black charcoal and cinnabar are all favored dyes. Today, commercial sealing waxes are available at book, gift and stationery stores. These will usually be in a stick form with a wick. To use them, light the wick just like a candle, then tilt at a 45 degree angle over the flap of the envelope. When enough wax has dripped onto the paper, impress the seal firmly, then pull it free. You have just added a hint of mystic elegance to your correspondence.

Sometimes wax seals are strong enough to survive the post office, but it may be wise to put the letter inside a padded envelope for mailing to make certain it arrives intact.

— DIKKI-JO MULLEN

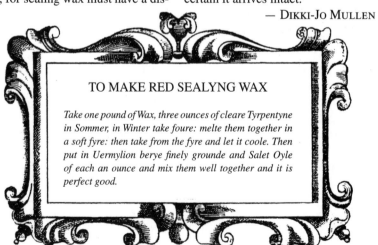

TO MAKE RED SEALYNG WAX

Take one pound of Wax, three ounces of cleare Tyrpentyne in Sommer, in Winter take foure: melte them together in a soft fyre: then take from the fyre and let it coole. Then put in Uermylion berye finely grounde and Salet Oyle of each an ounce and mix them well together and it is perfect good.

From *The Treasurie of Commodious Conceipts and Hidden Secrets*, by John Partridge, 1573

Circle of Fire

The ancient Norse myths preserved in Icelandic Eddic poems were splendidly translated by Irish author Padraic Colum in *The Children of Odin* published in 1920. The edition was replete with charming illustrations by Willy Pogany in Art Nouveau style. From that book we excerpt the tale of star-crossed lovers — Brynhild and Sigurd.

Brynhild. "To choose the heroes, and to give victory to those whom he willed to have victory, Odin had battle-maidens that went to the fields of war. Beautiful were those battle-maidens and fearless; wise were they also, for to them Odin showed the Runes of Wisdom. Valkyries, Choosers of the Slain, they were named. Youngest of all the battle-maidens was Brynhild. Nevertheless, to her Odin All-Father had shown more of the Runes than he had shown to any of her sisters....

"Doomed was Brynhild on the instant she went against Odin's will. A mortal woman she was now, and the Norns began to spin the thread of her mortal destiny... Odin said 'Is there aught thou wouldst have me bestow on thee in thy mortal life, Brynhild?' 'Naught save this,' Brynhild answered. 'That in my mortal life no one but a man without fear, the bravest hero in the world, may claim me for wife.' All-Father bowed his head in thought. 'It shall be as thou asked. Only he without fear shall come near thee'....

"Then on the top of the mountain that is called Hindfell he had a Hall built that faced south. Ten dwarfs built it of black stone. And when the Hall was built he put around it a wall of mounting and circling fire. He took a thorn of the Tree of Sleep and put it into the flesh of the battle-maiden. Then, with her helmet on her head and the breast-mail of the Valkyrie upon her, he lifted Brynhild in his arms and carried her through the wall of mounting and circling fire. He laid her upon a couch that was within the Hall. There she would lie in slumber until the hero who was without fear should ride through the flame and waken her to the life of a mortal woman."

Sigurd. "Before he came to warrior's age, Sigurd was known for his strength and his swiftness and for the fearlessness that shown around him like a glow....

Sigurd chose as his mount a grey horse, young and proud, with a great flowing mane named Grani.... He reclaimed Gram, the glorious sword of his forebears, and with it slayed a fearsome dragon. And it was the blood of the dragon that enabled Sigurd to understand the language of the birds.

"Deep in the forest, the birds sang of a Hall that was called the House of

Flame. All round the Hall there was a circle of fire through which none might pass. And within the Hall a maiden slept, and she was the wisest and the bravest and the most beautiful maiden in the world. Sigurd stood like a man enchanted listening to what the birds sang....

"The forest ways led him on and up a mountain-side. He came to a mountain-summit at last: Hindfell, where the trees fell away, leaving a place open to the sky and winds. On Hindfell was the House of Flame. Sigurd saw the walls black, and high, and all around them was a ring of fire. As he rode nearer he heard the roar of the mounting and circling fire. He sat on Grani, his proud horse, and for long he looked on the black walls and the flame that went circling around them.

"Then he rode Grani to the fire. Another horse would have been affrighted, but Grani remained steady under Sigurd. To the wall of fire they came, and Sigurd, who knew no fear, rode through it.

"Now he was in the court-yard of the Hall. No stir was there of man or hound or horse. Sigurd dismounted and bade Grani be still. He opened a door

and he saw a chamber with hangings on which was wrought the pattern of a great tree, a tree with three roots, and the pattern was carried across from one wall to the other. On a couch in the centre of the chamber one lay in slumber. Upon the head was a helmet and across the breast was a breastplate. Sigurd took the helmet off the head. Then over the couch fell a heap of woman's hair—wondrous, bright-gleaming hair. This was the maiden that the birds had told him of.

"He cut the fastenings of the breastplate with his sword, and he gazed long upon her. Beautiful was her face, but stern; like the face of one who subdues but may not be subdued. Beautiful and strong were her arms and her hands. Her mouth was proud, and over her closed eyes there were strong and beautiful brows.

"Her eyes opened, and she turned them and looked full upon Sigurd. 'Who art thou who hast awakened me?' she said.

'I am Sigurd, the son of Sigmund, of the Volsing race,' he answered.

'And thou didst ride through the ring of fire to me?'

'That did I.'"

SEDNA
star of the icy seas

A newly recognized planet twinkles at us from proximity to the constellation Cetus, the Whale. Sedna first greeted humanity as a whole during a transit through the zodiac sign of Taurus. Three times as far from the Sun as Pluto, Sedna corresponds with the New Millennium's many upsets, opportunities and changes. This outsider reveals that our solar system extends farther than we ever imagined. The new star of the day is a mysterious, shiny red planet, the largest object discerned circling our Sun since the discovery of Pluto in 1930. Sedna has an eccentric orbit. A single transit around the Sun takes 10,500 years, and because of its elliptical path it has not been this close to Earth since dinosaurs fought a losing battle with the Ice Age. Sedna remains in a single zodiac sign for 900 to 1,000 years, and little has changed on the face of this ancient one since the universe formed. The planet is very cold, with an estimated temperature on its face of 400 degrees below zero. From the planet's surface, the Sun appears only as a pale star offering little light or warmth.

Our new planetary neighbor has been aptly named for an Eskimo Sea Goddess, a key figure in the Inuit mythology of the frozen North. Sedna's mother and father were giants, and she was as beautiful as a star. But she grew more huge than either parent, and since food was scarce she was always ravenous. Her father, tired of complaints, married Sedna off to a mysterious hunter. He promised her a warm, magnificent nest and all the food she could eat. The couple set off on a boat, but soon he changed into a loon, or some say raven, and flew off to the Land of Birds with Sedna on his back. Her new home was cold and windy, with only fish to eat. Sedna was miserable.

Her father set out to rescue his daughter. Rowing home, the canoe was attacked by the Bird People. Fearing for his life, the father threw Sedna overboard into the icy waters. She grabbed the boat and held on. Her cowardly father cut off her fingers — and something magical happened. From Sedna's fingers came forth all the creatures of the northern seas: sea lions, whales, walrus, orcas, seal, salmon, polar bears. Her body grew fins and a fishtail, and for eons she has resided at the bottom of the sea, imprisoned by rocks. Friendly sea creatures comb her long hair. Sedna has lost her beauty and grown very old. But she exerts a marvelous power. The goddess punishes greedy hunters who kill more than they need — and blesses with plenty those who hunt in a virtuous way. Even now it is believed that Eskimo shamans may visit Sedna, although the trip is fraught with peril. The shaman must "pass through the realms of death and then cross the abyss where a wheel of ice spins eternally and a cauldron of seal meat stews endlessly. To return, he must cross another abyss on a bridge as narrow as a knife edge."

Hail Great Sedna
Old Food Basket of the Deep, bountiful and fierce
She Who commands Seal, Walrus, Whales and Polar Bear
Sedna of the Northern Deep, Mother of the Sea's Creatures.

Creatrix Who sustains the Inuit
She Who swims in the Icy Ocean
She Who is Guardian of All who honor Her
Sedna, strong abundant Hag of the Sea.

PROMETHEUS

The romance of fire inspired poets from earliest time. Four thousand years ago Egyptians hailed the coming of the Phoenix. The fabulous bird symbolized enduring life by suffering a fiery death only to arise again from its own ashes. The Homeric Hymn to Demeter tells how the goddess placed the infant Demophoön in the heart of the hearth fire to grant him everlasting life. Perhaps the most potent story of fire derives from Greek myth as told by Hesiod:

> *Zeus would not give the power of fire to the race*
> *of mortal men who live on earth. But Prometheus*
> *outwitted him and stole the far-seen gleam of*
> *unwearying fire in a hollow fennel stalk.*

Prometheus was a resourceful Titan who stole fire from the sun and gave it to humans. His deed infuriated Zeus, who had Prometheus chained to a rock and made to suffer unspeakable torture. His punishment would end only when he disclosed the identity of the woman who would bear the son destined to depose Zeus. It was a secret known only to the Titan and one he refused to disclose.

Prometheus would become an archetypal figure in Western culture—the defiant rebel, humanity's champion, refusing to bend to the will of a supreme power. Aeschylus, the great Greek dramatist, wrote of the Titan's nobility in *Prometheus Bound*. The Roman poet Ovid told the tale again some four hundred and fifty years later. Centuries passed before England's Shelley defined the hero in his preface to his lyrical drama, *Prometheus*

Unbound, as "the type of the highest perfection of moral and intellectual nature impelled by the purest and the truest motives to the best and noblest ends."

A giant gleaming statue of Prometheus dominates the plaza of Manhattan's Rockefeller Center. The bronze figure covered in gold leaf is by Paul Manship, a sculptor noted for his skill in expressing vitality and movement. The Fire Giver floats above a wide circular band upon which appear the twelve signs of the zodiac.

Manship often found inspiration in classical myths. His original sketches for the monument show a torch in the hero's right hand. The final version, however, adhers to Hesiod's words about preserving fire in the pithy center of a plant stem, a primitive way to carry fire from place to place. The noble character of the Titan is evident in the sculptor's tribute: *Prometheus brought the fire that hath proved to mortals a means to mighty ends.*

FIRE SIGNS

Astrology designates Aries, Leo and Sagittarius as fire signs. The three are categorized as masculine, aggressive and proud.

ARIES the Ram enjoys the gift of leadership. The first cardinal sign of the heavenly circle marks the advent of spring. Ariens never look back; their primary concern is always the road ahead. Audacious, daring to a fault, Aries demands attention.

LEO the Lion possesses the mighty sun's abstract nature: relentless, arrogant, dramatic — the fixed sign of summer heat. Leo's charm and dignity blend with a strong ego and dangerous volatility. Quick to anger and quick to forgive, the Lion's expansive quality needs careful tending.

SAGITTARIUS the Archer, the most benevolent of the fiery trio, typifies the peace and domesticity of the hearth. Yet take care, for strong passions spring from the glowing embers. A mutable sign defining the end of a season, the Archer offers resolute judgements — all decisons are final.

The Summoning

On a lonely beach in the mists of early spring, a young woman whose prince has not yet appeared can speed his coming with the help of a witch.

You'll need a small iron pot to hold a fiery coal, the fallen feather of a wild bird, a pure white stone to fit the palm of your hand, a silver cup. . . and a witch. Actually someone who loves you and sincerely wants your wish to come true; your mother, sister, or best friend can assume the role of the witch. Make sure that the one you choose is not only in sympathy with the proceedings, but able to achieve and sustain deep concentration.

At ebb tide draw a circle in the wet sand of a diameter to match your height. Mark the cardinal points by putting the iron pot with its lighted coal at the South. Thrust the shaft of the feather symbolizing Air at the West. Place the stone representing Earth at the North, and the silver cup filled with Water from the sea at the East. The witch stands in the center of the circle and you, the maiden, at the perimeter. (*Both face East.*)

Take time now to collect your thoughts. Center your being by breathing deeply until you feel balanced and sure. Raise your right arm when you are ready to begin. (*Both turn and face South.*)

WITCH: In the Season of Fire, by the grace of a Young Moon, we meet on hallowed ground to summon the mate of this most cherished child.

MAIDEN: *(Stooping to blow the coal into glowing fire)* I will delight him with fiery thought, surprise him with silence, and brighten all of his days.

WITCH: Even now he comes.

(Both turn and face West)

MAIDEN: *(plucking feather from the sand and tossing it to the wind)* I will honor him with trust and hold his love as lightly as the wind does this feather.

WITCH: Even now he comes.

(Both turn and face North)

MAIDEN: *(holding the stone in cupped hands)* I will comfort him with the old wisdom of the earth while blessing its continuing cycles.

WITCH: Even now he comes.

(Both turn and face East)

MAIDEN: *(Anointing forehead, lips, and heart with sea water)* : I will love him with the force, the depth, and the steadfastness of the sea.

WITCH: Even now he comes.

MAIDEN: *(Stretch your arms out before you and then high over your head)*

WITCH: The rite is ended.

Shake the coal from the pot. Pour the remaining water over the coal and cover it with sand. Erase all evidence of the ceremony but keep the white stone as a remembrance of the day.

It's wise to learn the words by heart and practice the procedure beforehand. And once a ritual has begun, under no circumstances interrupt or delay its completion.

Many cultures regard the ocean as a source of wisdom and that sandy stretch of shore where the tides cross back and forth a sacred and magical place. Here you may come to understand ancient truths, determine your fate, or perhaps set in motion the fulfillment of a haunting dream by performing the rite of summoning.

From *Love Charms* by Elizabeth Pepper

Questions & Answers

Q. Do you know of an effective but harmless spell to get rid of domestic friction ranging from violent rage to sullen silence?

D.L.T.
London, England

A. This spell comes from the diary of a Victorian witch.

GOOD RIDDANCE

Carefully wash a wide-mouth jar with a screw-on lid in hot sudsy water. Rinse, dry, and leave open to the air to collect whatever anger or resentment is present. You'll need a white candle, a small sheet of heavy paper, black pen, black silk thread, sea salt, and powdered frankincense and myrrh. Light the candle and write:

By these words I bind all evil thoughts and deeds now manifesting within this dwelling place. So shall it be!

Roll up the paper and firmly tie it with black thread. Fill the jar with sea salt, frankincense and myrrh powders. Insert the scroll of paper in the center so it is completely hidden from sight. Close the jar and drip white wax around the edge of the lid to seal it. You may keep the jar in a hidden place or bury it deep in the earth.

Q. What is the correct way to anoint a candle?

R.B.
Walden, New York

A. Many witches use this method. Place the candle on a white napkin folded in a triangle, its apex and wick pointing north. With your forefinger, dip the appropriate oil from its vessel and anoint the center of the candle. Lightly spread the oil to the north (wick end) and then back to the base while you chant aloud your intention.

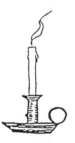

Q. About *Drawing down the Moon:* As I've looked through past Almanacs I see that it happens around the same time every year, and only occurs once a year. Can you tell me what this ritual is for, and, of course, hints on carrying it out in the proper way.

S.H.
Houston, Texas

A. The traditional time of year to perform the rite is at the Full Moon closest to Midsummer Night, the summer solstice. When the Moon is high, go to an open space carrying a small bowl of spring water. Capture the Moon's reflection in the bowl and hold it as steady as possible in both hands for a slow and silent count to nine. Close your eyes and while you keep the image of the Moon in your mind, drink the water to the last drop.

The purpose of the ritual is to renew psychic energy.

Q. I'm moving into a new apartment next month, and the previous tenant had been living there for years. The atmosphere is depressing. Is there any kind of ritual work I could do to eliminate whatever influences are lingering around?

K.M.W.
Boston, Massachusetts

A. An old tried and true recipe for puriflying an atmosphere is to place a sliced tooth of garlic on a saucer for the last three days of the waning moon. It will absorb any negative influence persisting in the room. Cover the garlic with common salt before disposing of it. Take care not to touch it.

Q. I found a wonderful piece of willow wood from which I've fashioned a wand. In looking up the runes to mark on it I found:

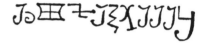

However, I am unable to find the meaning of this inscription. Can you track it down for me?

E.W.
Lanham, Maryland

A. It means "sacred instrument" as given in *True Black Magic*, a grimoire (magical grammar), published in Rome in 1750. The wand to be so marked is described in the text as of virgin hazel (one year's growth) and cut at sunrise on a Wednesday in the hour of Mercury. Operations of ceremonial magic defined in Europe during the Renaissance must be followed to the letter to be effective.

Your willow wand belongs to the Moon and may be used as a "wishing rod" if you choose. Such a tool does not serve the purpose of harmful magic, and may be marked on the handle with four dots and three crosses in this manner:

• X • X • X •

Space the dots so as to fit your fingertips when you hold the wand.

Q. Can you tell me where the phrases "merry meet, merry part" and "Blessed Be" originated? Are they really old and long connected with witchcraft or just the inspiration of modern writers on the subject?

B.E.T.
New York, New York

A. An early English translation of German poet Goethe's *Faust* includes the following lines from the "Chorus of Witches":

> *On to the Brocken the witches*
> *are flocking—*
> *Merry meet—merry part—*
> *How they gallop and drive.*

A common phrase in 18th-century England, its association with the Craft is based solely on this poem.

Regarding "Blessed Be": The final paragraph in Gerald Gardner's book *Witchcraft Today* is probably the source. It reads: "Having said all I am permitted to say, I must now finish. I hope that this book will have been of interest to you, the reader, and as the witches say to each other—BLESSED BE." The popular phrase more than likely was coined by Gardner.

Helena Petrovna Blavatsky

Q. May 8th is always marked on your calendar page as White Lotus Day. Is it ancient or a witches' holiday that I've never heard of?

F.C.
Atlanta, Georgia

A. Helena Blavatsky died on May 8, 1891. The following year White Lotus Day was inaugurated to honor her memory. Madame Blavatsky founded the Theosophical Society, wrote *The Secret Doctrine* and *Isis Unveiled*, and is considered by many to be the most influential occultist of modern times.

Any questions? We answer as many as possible. Send to The Witches' Almanac, PO Box 1292, Newport, RI 02840 or email to witchesal@yahoo.com. Published letters may be edited for brevity. We will identify by initials only, city and state.

Gerald Brousseau Gardner

ADAGES

Household sayings we hear as children often become words of power that echo through time to guide our daily living. The principles of wisdom and truth set forth in these concise verbal expressions represent the basic concepts of magical practice.

The moving tide reveals the truth.

Joy is as inevitable as sorrow.

Secrets are best hidden in plain sight.

Evil done returns to the sender thrice.

Good done comes back one hundredfold.

Thoughts are things.

Leave hatred to those not strong enough to love.

Guard hope as you would the last flame.

To judge is to harm.

A will unused is a will undone.

The weak shape their own destiny.

As above, so below.

If you would learn to dance, never watch your feet.

There is but one of you in all of time.

You cannot learn what you think you already know.

A creature in distress is a sacred object.

Pure ends require pure means.

Only you know what's good for you.

Need not who needs not thee.

Enough is better than too much.

The guilty flee where no one pursues.

Lose not substance for shadow.

The Da Vinci Spellbinder

Late-night in the Grand Gallery of the Louvre. A mountainous albino monk shoots Jacques Saunière, a 76-year-old curator. The victim staggers, mortally wounded. "Pain is good, monsieur," says the attacker. Then he is gone. The dying man uses his last agonizing moments to convey a message: *I must pass on the secret. An unbroken chain of knowledge.* And that brings us to the third page of *The Da Vinci Code*, a novel that whizzes along at the literary speed of light. From the beginning we know whodunnit; we burn to know whyhedunnit.

Published in 2003, the book became an immediate sensation, roosting for an incredible length of time on bestseller lists, emulating the habits of Harry Potter. Apparently mainstream readers as well as lovers of the arcane are eating up esoteric literature with a spoon. If you have not already caught up with this superb thriller, consider yourself nudged in its direction. I couldn't put it down, and I can't believe I just wrote that.

Author Dan Brown, Amherst grad and former English teacher, has published three previous novels: *Digital Fortress*, *Deception Point* and *Angels and Demons*. The books resonate with interests that derive from Brown's own life; his father a math professor, his mother an expert in sacred music, his wife an art historian. Themes Brown touched on throughout the earlier novels amplify in *Da Vinci* and their range is mind boggling: feminist religious principles, fanatical sects, symbols, cryptograms, codes, anagrams, puzzles, inventions, conspiracies, the Holy Grail, a pagan fertility cult, a ritual sex orgy, medieval history, secrets of European churches and cathedrals, and serio-prankish symbolism in artworks of Leonardo Da Vinci. Fact and fiction interweave within the thriller structure and its time-honored matrix of danger and chases. Most chapters are only a few pages long, and the prose is so elegantly taut you sense that if an overzealous editor cut one word the book would unravel like a sweater with a pulled thread.

Da Vinci turns up at once in the plot. The stricken curator has arranged himself nude within a drawn circle, arms and legs spread-eagled, a pentagram drawn on his torso — a living cryptogram of the artist's most famous drawing. Next to his body the dying man has scrawled a numerical code and *"0, Draconian devil! Oh, lame saint."*

The message concludes, *"Find Robert Langdon."* The enigmatic message puts the plot on the fast track from clue to clue in tracking down the murderer.

The protagonist, Robert Langdon, is a Harvard professor of religious symbology. Asked about the significance of the pentacle, he launches into an explanation that embraces a surprising goddess connection: "One of the oldest symbols on earth. Used over four thousand years before Christ... Early religion was based on the divine order of Nature. The goddess Venus and the planet Venus were one and the same. The goddess had a place in the nighttime sky and was known by many names — Venus, the Eastern Star, Ishtar, Astarte — all of them powerful female concepts." Langdon goes on to explain that as an astrology student he had been "stunned to learn that Venus traced a *perfect* pentacle across the ecliptic sky every eight years. So astonished were the ancients to observe the phenomenon that Venus and her pentacle became symbols of perfection, beauty, and the cyclic qualities of sexual love. As a tribute to the magic of Venus, the Greeks used her eight-year cycle to organize their Olympic Games."

Sophie Neveu, a French cryptologist, is Langdon's co-protagonist. They are madly in love with each other's brains, although actual romance may be simmering on the back burner.

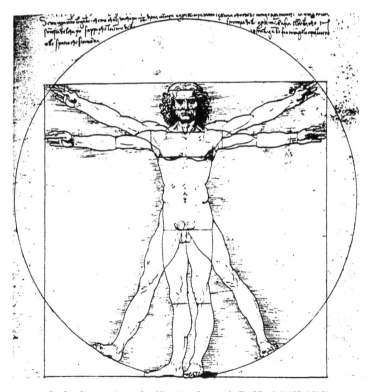

Study of proportions after Vitruvius, Leonardo Da Vinci (1452-1519)

Throughout the book they run and hide, hide and run. The couple is relentlessly pursued by Capitaine Bezu Fache, a French police pitbull, convinced that Langdon is the killer. The fleeing pair are aided and abetted by an English expat, Sir Leigh Teabing, whose impressive name I can't stop reading as Teabag.

The plot zigs and zags through architectural sites in France, England and Scotland chateaux, churches, cathedrals. Throughout Brown dishes out facts; some speed the plot, some indulge the author's sense of fun. We learn that if you follow the perimeter of the horseshoe-shaped Louvre, you will take a three-mile walk. Why mathematicians consider 1.618 numerical perfection. That in any beehive on the planet the ratio of female to male bees is always constant.

A secret society, the Priory of Sion, figures largely in the plot, and a preface assures the reader of the organization's present reality. It was founded in 1099, and members once included Da Vinci, Botticelli, and Sir Isaac Newton. Saumière has sacrificed his life to safeguard the Priory's sacred secret — the location of a hugely important religious relic hidden for centuries. Langdon and Neveu pursue the Priory relic, matching wits with a sinister, shadowy powerbroker from Opus Dei, a controversial prelature of the Vatican real enough to occupy a building on Lexington Avenue in New York.

The heart of the mystery must not be divulged. But Brown states that the book deals with "The greatest conspiracy of the past two thousand years." And the feminist doctrine develops as the plot thickens. "Two thousand years ago we lived in a world of Gods and Goddesses," the author points out. "Today we live in a world solely of Gods. Women in most cultures have been stripped of their spiritual power. The novel touches on questions of how and why this shift occurred."

A certain amount of controversy has exploded around Brown's unconventional interpretations of abiding religious icons. I can't imagine, for instance, that Mel Gibson would be much of a fan. Neither is a priest at the Church of Saint-Sulpice in Paris, where a key scene takes place. Father Paul Roumanet has put up a sign that virtually bristles with indignation: "Contrary to fanciful allegations in a recent best-selling novel, this is not a vestige of a pagan temple." Although as one of the author's oddity offerings, Brown reveals that the Marquis de Sade was baptized there.

— BARBARA STACY

Something to cheer about...

The Element Encyclopedia of 5000 Spells by Judika Illes is subtitled "The ultimate reference book for the magical arts." And indeed it is all that and more. Enormous (1,108) pages, elegant, comprehensive, this volume brings to mind the 1950's *Gourmet Cookbooks*, that so enhanced cuisine in America. Like those vintage examples, we can look ahead fifty years and imagine

Illes' contribution will be as soiled, smudged and tattered as those classics are today.

Magic's goal is to improve the quality of life, and this is a book destined to do that with every spell you would ever want. In a remarkable range of space and time, we find spells from every occult tradition on the planet. Judika Illes is a delightful guide as we move from Hungary to the Ozarks, China to Haiti.

In the 2002/3 edition of *The Witches' Almanac* we mentioned the mysterious Vila, witch of the wood. We meet her again here in a chapter called "Spells for Justice":

VILA JUSTICE SPELL
Not all issues of justice are legal matters. The vila are fierce, beautiful Eastern European spirits who seek justice for injured, humiliated, and harmed women and animals. They are old, wild forest spirits and may not be verbally articulate.

1. Communicate your pain and passion to the vila by dancing.

2. For utmost power, dance outdoors;

however it is your passion and the depths of your psychic wound that calls and activates their power.

3. Request that they provide justice for you; dance until you drop, then leave your burden with the vila.

4. Should pain and feelings of injustice become overwhelming, repeat as needed.

There's more about the Vila in "Spirit Summoning Spells." Illes asks her readers: *Why would you wish to summon them? Because the Vila are masters and sometimes teachers of shape-shifting magic.*

Southernwood is one of the most neglected herbs in magic. It is excellently referenced in no less than three chapters. From "Protection Spells":

In medieval Europe, southernwood was considered one of the most potent spiritual antidotes to malicious magical workings. Southernwood belongs to the Artemisia family, sacred plants dedicated to Artemis. It is closely related to its more notorious cousin wormwood; its name is a corruption of "southern wormwood."

For purposes of protection:
- *Carry in a charm bag*
- *Place under one's pillow*
- *Post it in your house*

In "Theft, Lost Objects, and Missing Persons" there's a southernwood spell to protect against thieves: *Carry a twig as a talisman, and place southernwood twigs beside items requiring protection.*

Last but not least: From "Love Magic":

SOUTHERNWOOD SPELL
Southernwood's nickname is "lad's love," perhaps reflecting its reputation as a tool for magical seduction. Place it under the mattress to arouse passion and performance.

Judika Illes' tribute to Hecate occurs in the chapter on summoning spirits and it provides a primary theme — the very nature of the entire book:
Hecate, Queen of Witches, pre-eminent deity of the ancient nation of Caria, Matron of Midwives, and psychopomp

maintains office hours only at night: formal petitions and invitations must be offered after dark. A particularly ancient spirit, the only source of illumination she favors is fire.

Summon Hecate at night by a three-way crossroads. Ideally, light your way with a mullein torch. Offer her garlic, lavender, and honey. If you have a dog, bring it with you. Keep an eye on the dog; it's likely to perceive Hecate, who adores dogs, before you do. Why would you wish to contact Hecate? Because she can teach you to do anything in this book. Because she can grant you enhanced psychic powers, fertility, romance, protection, freedom from illness, and magical restitution for any crime committed against you.

We might wish the publisher had chosen a less awkward title, but never mind. Witches will call this Judika's Spellbook for decades to come.

— ELIZABETH PEPPER

Keepers of the Flame

Interviews with Elders of
Traditional Witchcraft in America

by Morganna Davies and Aradia Lynch

Many Traditional Witches have deliberately avoided all the fanfare and media hype that some who call themselves "witches" seem to covet. Some have preferred to remain anonymous, quietly practicing their Craft and passing the Tradition on to their students. These Elders are growing older and the torches are being passed to a new generation.

This book is not *about* the Elders, it is a record of their opinions, views, comments and ideas of what the Craft was, what it is today, and what they think it will be in the future.

Morganna Davies is an Alexandrian Priestess and was a member of one of the early covens in the United States. Aradia Lynch is a High Priestess of the New England Coven of Traditionalist Witches.

Including interviews with:

- Elizabeth Pepper, author of *The Witches' Almanac*
- Raymond Buckland, author of *The Complete Book of Witchcraft*
- Hanz Holzer, author, and a leading authority on psychic phenomena
- Leo Martello, author, and leading "personality" who won civil rights for Witches in America.

$20.95 – 216 pages

Available at OlympianPress.com/keepers.html

Order your copy now!

Name: _____

Address: _____

_____

Olympian Press, PO Box 29182, Providence, RI 02909 Phone: 401-331-8576

The Rede
of the Wiccae

Adriana Porter, Gwen Thompson
and the Birth of a Tradition of Witchcraft

by Robert Mathiesen and Theitic

This is a tale told by Gwen Thompson about her grandmother, Adriana Porter, and how she came to be the last carrier of her ancestral Tradition of Witchcraft.

The information was researched by Robert Mathiesen, a medieval philologist and professor at Brown University, and Theitic, an Elder in the Tradition that Gwen Thompson founded.

*Investigating a Family Tradition
of the Craft*
Gwen Thompson's Grandmother Tale

Who was Adriana Porter?
The course of Adriana Porter's life
and her ancestors in Salem, 1692

*What could Adriana Porter
have known?*
The persistence of Ancestral Traditions

Magic and the
Occult Sciences in old New England

Bluenose Folk-Magic at Yarmouth

Magic, Occultism and Alternative
Religion in Boston and vicinity

*A Closer Look at
The Rede of the Wiccae*

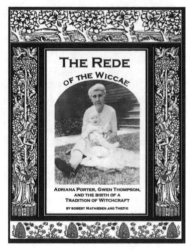

$22.95 – 200 pages
Available at
OlympianPress.com/keepers.html

FULL MOON NAMES

Students of occult literature soon learn the importance of names. From Ra to Rumpelstiltskin, the message is clear—names hold unusual power.

The tradition of naming full Moons was recorded in an English edition of The *Shepherd's Calendar*, published in the first decade of the 16th century.

Aries—Seed. Sowing season and symbol of the start of the new year.

Taurus—Hare. The sacred animal was associated in Roman legends with springtime and fertility.

Gemini—Dyad. The Latin word for a pair refers to the twin stars of the constellation Castor and Pollux.

Cancer—Mead. During late June and most of July the meadows, or meads, were mowed for hay.

Leo—Wort. When the sun was in Leo the worts (from the Anglo-Saxon wyrt-plant) were gathered to be dried and stored.

Virgo — Barley. Persephone, virgin goddess of rebirth, carries a sheaf of barley as symbol of the harvest.

Libra — Blood. Marking the season when domestic animals were sacrificed for winter provisions.

Scorpio — Snow. Scorpio heralds the dark season when the Sun is at its lowest and the first snow flies.

Sagittarius — Oak. The sacred tree of the Druids and the Roman god Jupiter is most noble as it withstands winter's blasts.

Capricorn—Wolf. The fearsome nocturnal animal represents the "night" of the year. Wolves were rarely seen in England after the 12th century.

Aquarius — Storm. A storm is said to rage most fiercely just before it ends, and the year usually follows suit.

Pisces — Chaste. The antiquated word for pure reflects the custom of greeting the new year with a clear soul.

Libra's Full Moon occasionally became the Wine Moon when a grape harvest was expected to produce a superior vintage.

America's early settlers continued to name the full Moons. The influence of the native tribes and their traditions is readily apparent.

AMERICAN	Colonial	Native
Aries / April	Pink, Grass, Egg	Green Grass
Taurus / May	Flower, Planting	Shed
Gemini / June	Rose, Strawberry	Rose, Make Fat
Cancer / July	Buck, Thunder	Thunder
Leo / August	Sturgeon, Grain	Cherries Ripen
Virgo / September	Harvest, Fruit	Hunting
Libra / October	Hunter's	Falling Leaf
Scorpio / November	Beaver, Frosty	Mad
Sagittarius / December	Cold, Long Night	Long Night
Capricorn / January	Wolf, After Yule	Snow
Aquarius / February	Snow, Hunger	Hunger
Pisces / March	Worm, Sap, Crow	Crow, Sore Eye

from *Moon Lore*

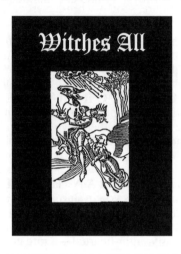

MAGIC CHARMS FROM A TO Z
A treasury of amulets, talismans, fetishes and other lucky objects compiled by the staff of *The Witches' Almanac*. An invaluable guide for all who respond to the call of mystery and enchantment.

LOVE CHARMS
Love has many forms, many aspects. Ceremonies performed in witchcraft celebrate the joy and the blessings of love. Here is a collection of love charms to use now and ever after.

MAGICAL CREATURES
Mystic tradition grants pride of place to many members of the animal kingdom. Some share our life. Others live wild and free. Still others never lived at all, springing instead from the remarkable power of human imagination.

ANCIENT ROMAN HOLIDAYS
The glory that was Rome awaits you in Barbara Stacy's classic presentation of a festive year in pagan times. Here are the gods and goddesses as the Romans conceived them, accompanied by the annual rites performed in their worship. Scholarly, light-hearted—a rare combination.

CELTIC TREE MAGIC
Robert Graves in *The White Goddess* writes of the significance of trees in the old Celtic lore. *Celtic Tree Magic* is an investigation of the sacred trees in the remarkable Beth-Luis-Nion alphabet; their role in folklore, poetry, and mysticism.

MOON LORE
As both the largest and the brightest object in the night sky, and the only one to appear in phases, the Moon has been a rich source of myth for as long as there have been myth-makers.

MAGIC SPELLS AND INCANTATIONS
Words have magic power. Their sound, spoken or sung, has ever been a part of mystic ritual. From ancient Egypt to the present, those who practice the art of enchantment have drawn inspiration from a treasury of thoughts and themes passed down through the ages.

LOVE FEASTS
Creating meals to share with the one you love can be a sacred ceremony in itself. With the witch in mind, culinary adept Christine Fox offers magical menus and recipes for every month in the year.

RANDOM RECOLLECTIONS I, II, III, IV
Pages culled from the original (no longer available) issues of *The Witches' Almanac,* published annually throughout the 1970's, are now available in a series of tasteful booklets. A treasure for those who missed us the first time around; keepsakes for those who remember.

Order form on overleaf

Order Form

Each edition of *The Witches' Almanac* is unique.
Limited numbers of previous years' editions are available.

____2005 - 2006 The Witches' Almanac @ $8.95_____

____2004 - 2005 The Witches' Almanac @ $8.95_____

____2003 - 2004 The Witches' Almanac @ $8.95_____

____2002 - 2003 The Witches' Almanac @ $7.95_____

____2001 - 2002 The Witches' Almanac @ $7.95_____

____2000 - 2001 The Witches' Almanac @ $7.95_____

____1999 - 2000 The Witches' Almanac @ $7.95_____

____1998 - 1999 The Witches' Almanac @ $6.95_____

____1997 - 1998 The Witches' Almanac @ $6.95_____

____1996 - 1997 The Witches' Almanac @ $6.95_____

____1995 - 1996 The Witches' Almanac @ $6.95_____

____1994 - 1995 The Witches' Almanac @ $5.95_____

____1993 - 1994 The Witches' Almanac @ $5.95_____

____Celtic Tree Magic @ $7.95_____

____Love Charms @ $6.95_____

____Random Recollection I @ $3.95_____

____Random Recollection II @ $3.95_____

____Random Recollection III @ $3.95_____

____Random Recollection IV @ $3.95_____

____A Book of Days @ $15.95_____

____Moon Lore @ $7.95_____

____Love Feasts @ $6.95_____

____Ancient Roman Holidays @ $6.95_____

____Magic Charms from A to Z @ $12.95_____

____Magical Creatures @ $12.95_____

____Magic Spells and Incantations @ $12.95_____

____Witches' All @ $13.95_____

Shipping and handling charges:
One book: $3.00
each additional book
add $1.00

Send your
name and
address along
with a check or money order
payable in U. S. funds or credit
card details to:
The Witches' Almanac, Ltd.
PO Box 1292, Newport, RI 02840-9998

*Subtotal*_____

*Shipping & handling*_____

*Sales tax (RI orders only)*_____

*Total*_____